Word
Made Simple

Made Simple *Computer Books*

● easy to follow   ● jargon free   ● practical   ● task based   ● easy steps

Thousands of people have already discovered that the **MADE SIMPLE** series gives them what they want *fast!* These are the books for you if you want to **learn quickly what's essential** and **how** to do things with a particular piece of software. Many delighted readers have written, telephoned and e-mailed us about the **Made Simple Series** of Computer books. Comments have included:

● "Clear, concise and well laid out"
● "Ideal for the first time user."
● "Clear, accurate, well presented, jargon free, well targeted."
● "Easy to follow to perform a task."
● "I haven't found any other books worth recommending until these."

This **best selling** series is in your **local bookshop now**, or in case of difficulty, contact:

Heinemann Publishers, Oxford, P.O.Box 381,Oxford OX2 8EJ.
Tel 01865 314300. Fax 01865 314091. Credit card sales 01865 314627.

Series titles:

Excel for Windows	Stephen Morris	0 7506 2070 6
Lotus 1-2-3 (DOS)	Ian Robertson	0 7506 2066 8
MS-DOS	Ian Sinclair	0 7506 2069 2
MS-Works for Windows	P. K. McBride	0 7506 2065 X
Windows 3.1	P. K. McBride	0 7506 2072 2
Word for Windows	Keith Brindley	0 7506 2071 4
WordPerfect (DOS)	Stephen Copestake	0 7506 2068 4
Access for Windows	Moira Stephen	0 7506 2309 8
The Internet	P.K.McBride	0 7506 2311 X
Quicken for Windows	Stephen Copestake	0 7506 2308 X
WordPerfect for Windows	Keith Brindley	0 7506 2310 1
Lotus 123 (5.0) for Windows	Stephen Morris	0 7506 2307 1
Multimedia	Simon Collin	0 7506 2314 4
Pageplus for Windows	Ian Sinclair	0 7506 2312 8
Powerpoint	Moira Stephen	0 7506 2420 5
Hard Drives	Ian Robertson	0 7506 2313 6
Windows 95	P.K. McBride	0 7506 2306 3
WordPro	Moira Stephen	0 7506 2626 7
Office 95	P.K. McBride	0 7506 2625 9
The Internet for Windows 95	P.K.McBride	0 7506 2835 9
Word for Windows 95	Keith Brindley	0 7506 2815 4
Excel for Windows 95	Stephen Morris	0 7506 2816 2
Internet Resources	P.K.McBride	0 7506 2836 7
Powerpoint for Windows 95	Moira Stephen	0 7506 2817 0
Microsoft Networking	P.K.McBride	0 7506 2837 5
Designing Internet Home Pages	Lilian Hobbs	0 7506 2941 X
Access for Windows 95	Moira Stephen	0 7506 2818 9

Word
Made Simple

Keith Brindley

MADE SIMPLE
BOOKS

Made Simple
An imprint of Butterworth-Heinemann Ltd
Linacre House, Jordan Hill, Oxford OX2 8DP

⟨R A member of the Reed Elsevier plc group

OXFORD LONDON BOSTON
MUNICH NEW DELHI SINGAPORE SYDNEY
TOKYO TORONTO WELLINGTON

First published 1994
Reprinted 1994,1995 (twice), 1996

British Library Cataloguing in Publication Data
A catalogue record for this book is available from the British
Library

ISBN 0 7506 2071 4

Typeset and produced by Co-publications, Loughborough
Set in Archetype, Cotswold Book and Gravity from Advanced
Graphics Limited
Icons designed by Sarah Ward © 1994
Printed and bound in Great Britain
by Scotprint, Musselburgh, Scotland

Contents

Preface

The computer is about as simple as a spacecraft, and who ever let an untrained spaceman loose? You pick up a manual that weighs more than your birth-weight, open it and find it's written in computerspeak. You see messages on the screen resembling some strange spy code and the thing even makes noises. No wonder you feel it's your lucky day if everything goes right. What do you do if everything goes wrong? Give up.

Training helps. Being able to type helps. Experience helps. This book helps, by providing training and assisting with experience. It can't help you if you always manage to hit the wrong keys, but it *can* tell you which are the right ones and what to do when you hit the wrong ones. After some time, even the dreaded manual will start to make sense, just because you at last know what the writers are wittering on about.

Computing is not black magic. You don't need luck or charms, just a bit of understanding. The problem is that the programs used nowadays *look* simple — but simply aren't. Most are crammed with features you don't need — but how do you know what you don't need? This book shows you what is essential and guides you through it. You will know how to make an action work and why. Less essential bits can wait — and once you start to use a program with confidence you can tackle those bits for yourself.

The writers of this series have all been through it. We know time is valuable, and you don't want to waste it. You don't buy books on computer topics to read jokes or be told you are a dummy. You want to find what you need — and be shown how to do it. Here, at last, you can.

1 The basics

Starting up

First operation you ever do when using Word is to start it up. Easiest method of doing this is to double-click the Word icon on your computer desktop. For a standard installation, this is in the Microsoft Office program group in Window's Program Manager.

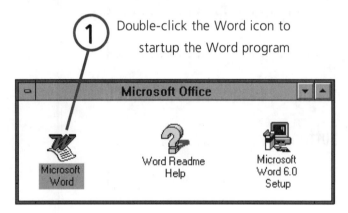

① Double-click the Word icon to startup the Word program

After starting, you will be presented first with the main Word window (shown right — for a completely new and unaltered program) followed quickly by the Tip of the Day (shown below). If your copy of Word has been adapted by any other user since installation your screen may display something a little different.

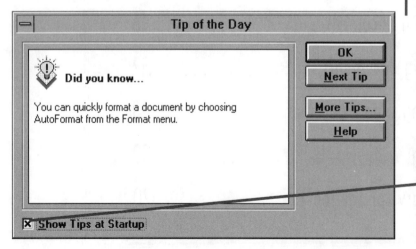

1 Double-click the Word icon in the Microsoft Office program group on the computer desktop

2 Alternatively, you can point and click on the Word icon, then choose **File↪Open** from the Program Manager menu bar, or press Enter

Tip:

If you use your computer only for word processing, you can setup to run Word each time you turn on your machine, by moving or copying Word's program icon to the Startup program group – see page 146

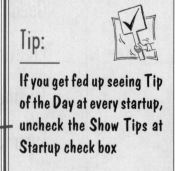

Tip:

If you get fed up seeing Tip of the Day at every startup, uncheck the Show Tips at Startup check box

2

Main features of a Word document window are shown below, but don't panic — they'll be looked at shortly. Soon you'll think Word is one of the easiest computer programs to get the hang of — and you'll be right.

The Word menu bar leads to commands available

Toolbars feature easily-clickable buttons which allow you to choose commands quickly

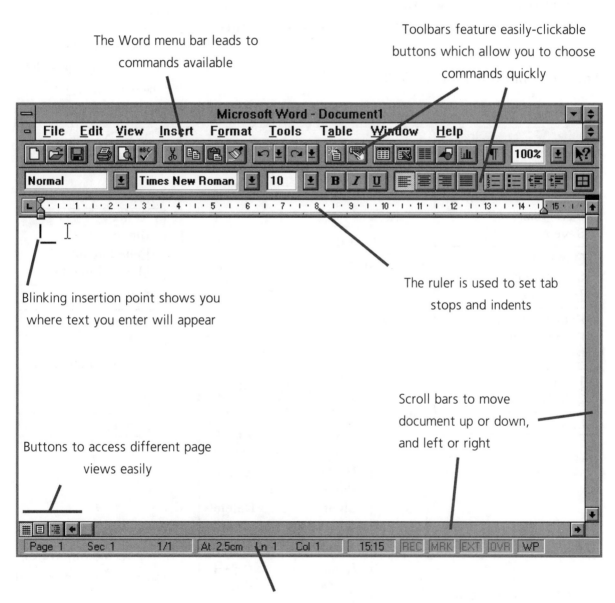

Blinking insertion point shows you where text you enter will appear

The ruler is used to set tab stops and indents

Scroll bars to move document up or down, and left or right

Buttons to access different page views easily

The status bar along the bottom gives details about the document in the window (see pages 22–23 for more details)

Word menus

Word has nine menus in its menu bar. They hold all the commands and tools available to any user of Word. While you don't (and that's just as well!) need to know what all these commands and tools are to get good results from Word, it's worth looking at all the menus to get an overall feel for what they are about — use this page as a reference.

The menu bar itself looks like this:

Basic steps:

1 To display a menu, click on its name in the menu bar

2 Alternatively, enter ⎡Alt⎤+ the menu's underlined letter

3 To remove a displayed menu, click anywhere else in the window

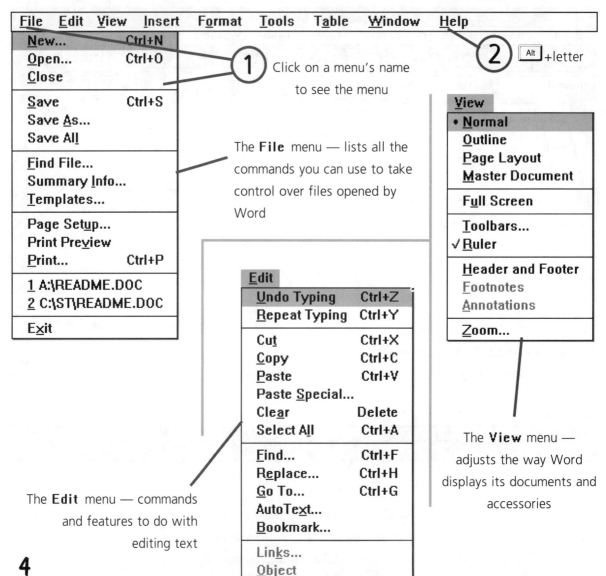

File   Edit   View   Insert   Format   Tools   Table   Window   Help

File	
New...	Ctrl+N
Open...	Ctrl+O
Close	
Save	Ctrl+S
Save As...	
Save All	
Find File...	
Summary Info...	
Templates...	
Page Setup...	
Print Preview	
Print...	Ctrl+P
1 A:\README.DOC	
2 C:\ST\README.DOC	
Exit	

1 Click on a menu's name to see the menu

2 ⎡Alt⎤+letter

The **File** menu — lists all the commands you can use to take control over files opened by Word

Edit	
Undo Typing	Ctrl+Z
Repeat Typing	Ctrl+Y
Cut	Ctrl+X
Copy	Ctrl+C
Paste	Ctrl+V
Paste Special...	
Clear	Delete
Select All	Ctrl+A
Find...	Ctrl+F
Replace...	Ctrl+H
Go To...	Ctrl+G
AutoText...	
Bookmark...	
Links...	
Object	

View	
• Normal	
Outline	
Page Layout	
Master Document	
Full Screen	
Toolbars...	
√ Ruler	
Header and Footer	
Footnotes	
Annotations	
Zoom...	

The **View** menu — adjusts the way Word displays its documents and accessories

The **Edit** menu — commands and features to do with editing text

4

Insert

Insert
Break...
Page Numbers...
Annotation
Date and Time...
Field...
Symbol...
Form Field...
Footnote...
Caption...
Cross-reference...
Index and Tables...
File...
Frame
Picture...
Object...
Database...

The **Insert** menu — used to place certain features over and above ordinary text into a document

The **Tools** menu — special features and controls

Format

Format
Font...
Paragraph...
Tabs...
Borders and Shading...
Columns...
Change Case...
Drop Cap...
Bullets and Numbering...
Heading Numbering...
AutoFormat...
Style Gallery...
Style...
Frame...
Picture...
Drawing Object...

Tools	
Spelling...	**F7**
Grammar...	
Thesaurus...	Shift+F7
Hyphenation...	
Language...	
Word Count...	
AutoCorrect...	
Mail Merge...	
Envelopes and Labels...	
Protect Document...	
Revisions...	
Macro...	
Customize...	
Options...	

The **Table** menu — controls aspects of tables within a document

Table
Insert Cells...
Delete Cells...
Merge Cells
Split Cells...
Select Row
Select Column
Select Table   Alt+Num 5
Table AutoFormat...
Cell Height and Width...
Headings
Convert Table to Text...
Sort...
Formula...
Split Table
√ Gridlines

The **Format** menu — the menu you use to apply styles and so on to your document

The **Window** menu — choose between documents and control how they are displayed

Window
New Window
Arrange All
Split
√1 Document1

The **Help** menu — how to how to?

Help
Contents
Search for Help on...
Index
Quick Preview
Examples and Demos
Tip of the Day...
WordPerfect Help...
Technical Support
About Microsoft Word...

Help, I'm drowning!

Basic steps:

Inevitably you will find there are times you don't know what you are doing. This happens whenever you are new (and, sometimes not-so-new) to a complex program like Word. Fortunately, Word has an incredibly useful — and even-more-incredibly comprehensive — on-line help system built-in to it. This comes in two parts:

● first there are ToolTips — little labels which show up when you point over any of the myriads of buttons Word has in its many toolbars (see over)

● second is Help — an easily accessible system in which you can locate help about any feature, command or topic in Word.

TOOLTIPS

1 Simply position your pointer over any button in any toolbar to see the button's name as a label

HELP

1 Choose **Help→Contents** to call up the Word Help Contents window

2 Click on any of the topics to get help

3 Further windows give help — cross-references may give you further help; simply click on a cross-reference to access help on it

(1) ToolTips give each button a name as the pointer passes over it

Take note:

As good as it is, ToolTips can become very irritating after a while. Turn it off by unchecking the Show ToolTips check box in the Toolbars dialog box (over)

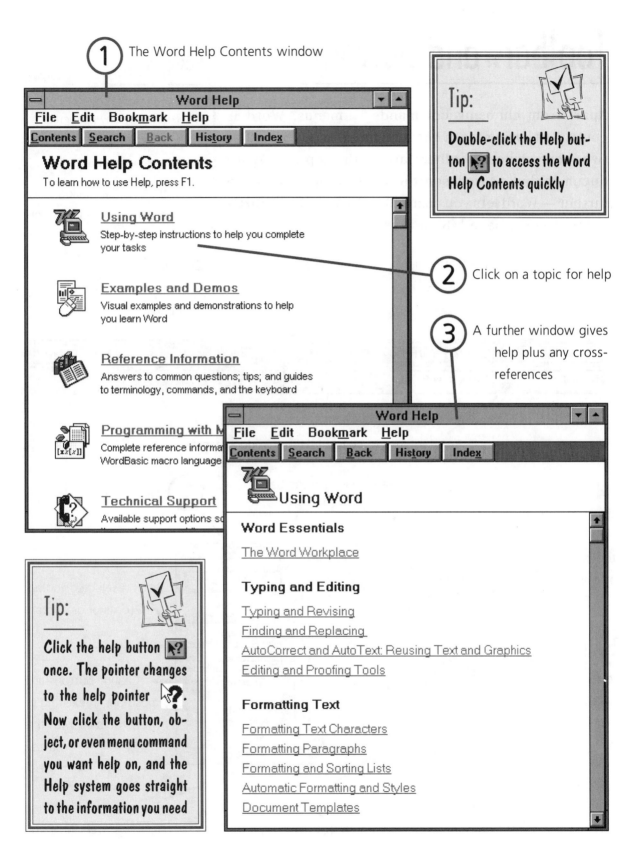

① The Word Help Contents window

Tip:

Double-click the Help button 🅺? to access the Word Help Contents quickly

Word Help

File Edit Bookmark Help

Contents | Search | Back | History | Index

Word Help Contents

To learn how to use Help, press F1.

Using Word
Step-by-step instructions to help you complete your tasks

② Click on a topic for help

③ A further window gives help plus any cross-references

Examples and Demos
Visual examples and demonstrations to help you learn Word

Reference Information
Answers to common questions; tips; and guides to terminology, commands, and the keyboard

Programming with M...
Complete reference informa...
WordBasic macro language

Technical Support
Available support options so...

Word Help

File Edit Bookmark Help

Contents | Search | Back | History | Index

Using Word

Word Essentials

The Word Workplace

Typing and Editing

Typing and Revising
Finding and Replacing
AutoCorrect and AutoText: Reusing Text and Graphics
Editing and Proofing Tools

Formatting Text

Formatting Text Characters
Formatting Paragraphs
Formatting and Sorting Lists
Automatic Formatting and Styles
Document Templates

Tip:

Click the help button 🅺? once. The pointer changes to the help pointer 🅺?. Now click the button, object, or even menu command you want help on, and the Help system goes straight to the information you need

Toolbars and buttons

Apart from choosing commands in menus, Word is controlled by on-screen buttons, found in toolbars. The two most obvious toolbars are at the top of a Word document but, as we'll see, there are others, too — and further — Word lets you customize them to your heart's content — see page 148 for more details.

Basic steps:

1 To display any particular toolbar, choose
   View → Toolbar

2 In the Toolbar dialog box, choose which toolbars you want displayed

3 Alternatively, use the shortcut — see the Tip opposite

The standard toolbar — buttons used
for common everyday tasks

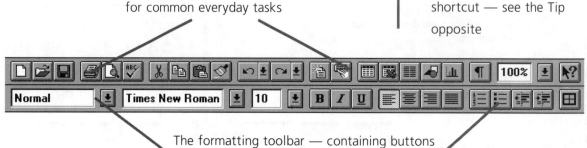

The formatting toolbar — containing buttons
you use to stylise text within documents

Create your own toolbars
with this button

(1) The Toolbars dialog box

Checked options
show those
toolbars displayed
at any time

(2) Check more
boxes to display
more toolboxes

Reset a selected toolbar
to its original state

Change buttons and
positions in existing or
new toolbars with this
button

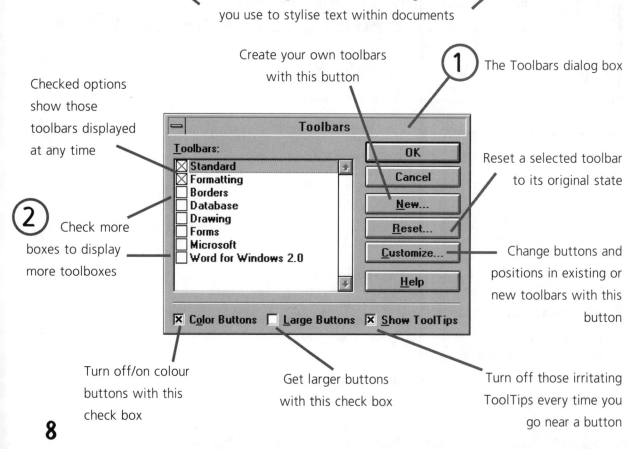

Turn off/on colour
buttons with this
check box

Get larger buttons
with this check box

Turn off those irritating
ToolTips every time you
go near a button

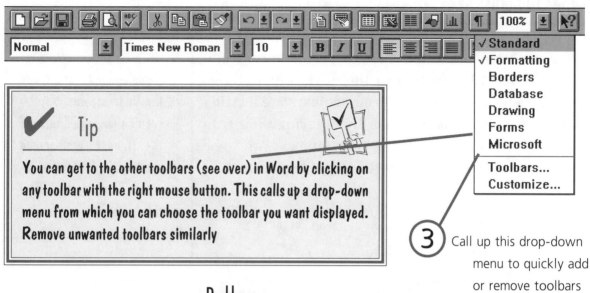

You can get to the other toolbars (see over) in Word by clicking on

Tip

You can get to the other toolbars (see over) in Word by clicking on any toolbar with the right mouse button. This calls up a drop-down menu from which you can choose the toolbar you want displayed. Remove unwanted toolbars similarly

(3) Call up this drop-down menu to quickly add or remove toolbars

Buttons

Buttons on toolbars are representative of their function. Here the standard and formatting toolbar buttons are listed, together with brief explanations.

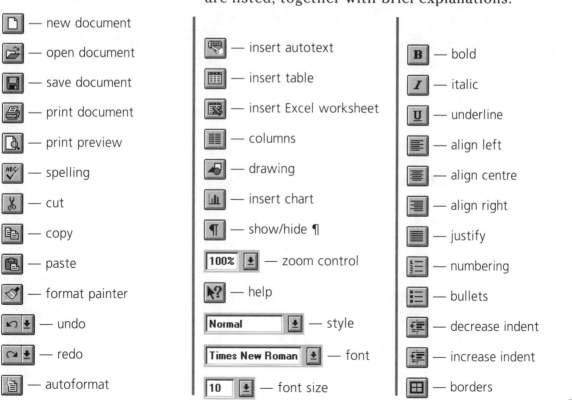

— new document
— open document
— save document
— print document
— print preview
— spelling
— cut
— copy
— paste
— format painter
— undo
— redo
— autoformat

— insert autotext
— insert table
— insert Excel worksheet
— columns
— drawing
— insert chart
— show/hide ¶
— zoom control
— help
— style
— font
— font size

— bold
— italic
— underline
— align left
— align centre
— align right
— justify
— numbering
— bullets
— decrease indent
— increase indent
— borders

Other toolbars:

All normal toolbars in Word are displayed here. While most are fixed in position in the document window, two: the Microsoft and the Forms toolbars are floating — that is, you can move them by dragging their title bars as you do any window in Windows. Any new toolbars you create for yourself (page 149) are floating too.

Tip:

If you've used Word 2, and the interface for Word 6 seems alien to you, turn off the Standard toolbar and use the Word 2 toolbar instead. That way you'll feel right at home

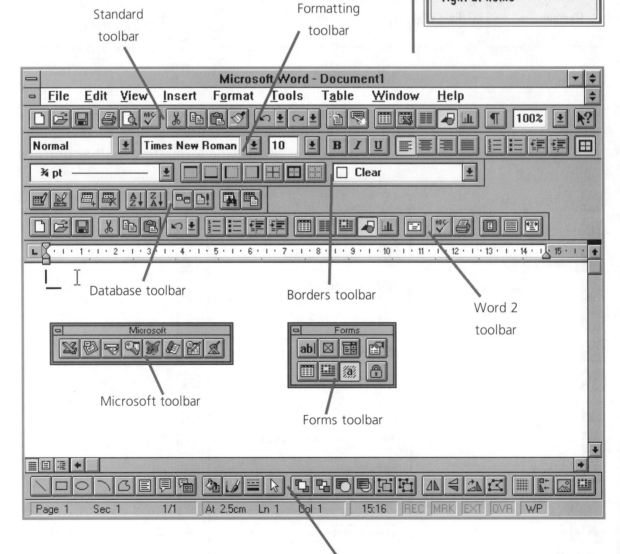

Standard toolbar

Formatting toolbar

Database toolbar

Borders toolbar

Word 2 toolbar

Microsoft toolbar

Forms toolbar

Drawing toolbar

Normal view

Word allows a number of views of your document — normal view is simply the one new documents usually default to. It's important to remember, though, that each view of a document makes no difference to what's actually in the document — it's just one way of looking at it.

Normal view

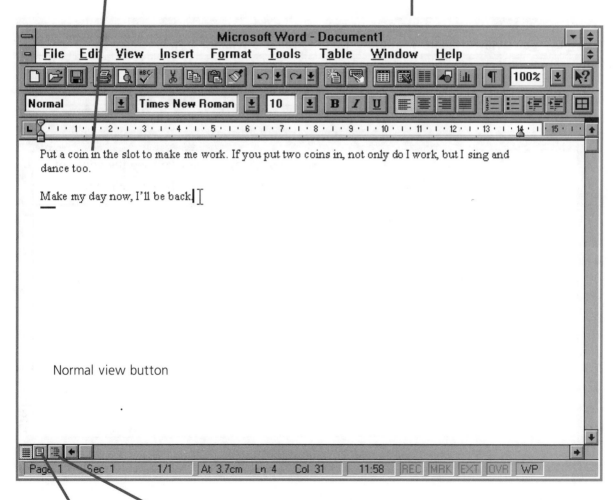

Normal view button

Page layout and outline view buttons

Page layout view

This view lets you see how the printed page will appear — *what you see is what you get* (WYSIWYG). Margins and borders around text are shown, as well as positions of graphics. This is a useful view to check the final appearance of your document before printing. However, general operation becomes slower, so should only really be used for this purpose.

Basic steps:

1 Choose **View ↳Page Layout**, or type [Alt]+[V] then [P], or (best) click the Page Layout button [≣] at the bottom left of your document window

(1) Page layout view

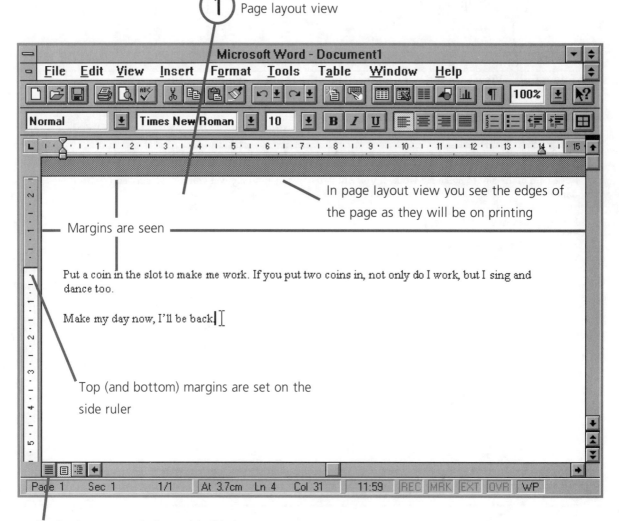

In page layout view you see the edges of the page as they will be on printing

Margins are seen

Put a coin in the slot to make me work. If you put two coins in, not only do I work, but I sing and dance too.

Make my day now, I'll be back.

Top (and bottom) margins are set on the side ruler

Get back to normal view with this button

Outline view

Outline view allows you to control how the various levels of heading and sub-headings in your document are displayed (or not displayed) and organised. It is the ideal method of re-arranging documents by moving parts of text long distances within the document, or changing the hierarchy of headings. See page 104 for details of outlining.

Basic steps:

1 Choose **View ↪ Outline**, or type ⌐Alt⌐+⌐V⌐ then ⌐O⌐, or (best) click the Outline button ▦ at the bottom left of your document window

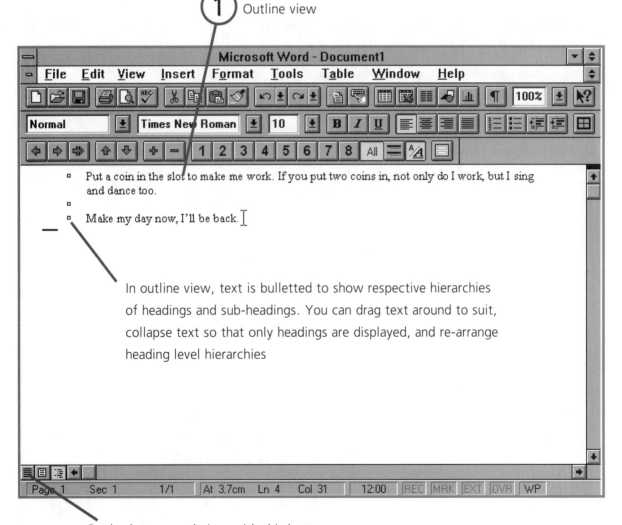

① Outline view

In outline view, text is bulletted to show respective hierarchies of headings and sub-headings. You can drag text around to suit, collapse text so that only headings are displayed, and re-arrange heading level hierarchies

Get back to normal view with this button

Full screen view

Word has a neat facility to get rid of all the on-screen clutter such as toolbars, menu line, scroll boxes and so on. Full screen view can improve your outlook on, say, a small monitor screen, yet you can still get back to normal view with just the click of a mouse.

Tip:

You can still access individual menus by typing `Alt`+the menu's underlined letter eg, `Alt`+`F` displays the File menu

Basic steps:

1 Choose **View ↪ Full Screen**, or type `Alt`+`V` then `U`. The screen display changes to full screen view — there is nothing on the screen except text or graphic elements you have entered, and the Full Screen toolbar in the bottom-right of the screen

Full screen view

Put a coin in the slot to make me work. If you put two coins in, not only do I work, but I sing and dance too.

Make my day now. I'll be back. ⌷

To get back to normal view, click the full screen button on the full screen toolbar.

Zooming

You can magnify or reduce part of a document page in Word, to get a close up or overall view of the page. This is known as zooming

Basic steps:

1 Click on the down arrow of the zoom control button of the standard toolbar

2 From the resultant drop-down menu, choose your desired zoom percentage

3 As an alternative you can choose **View → Zoom**, to call up the Zoom dialog box, and select zoom value there

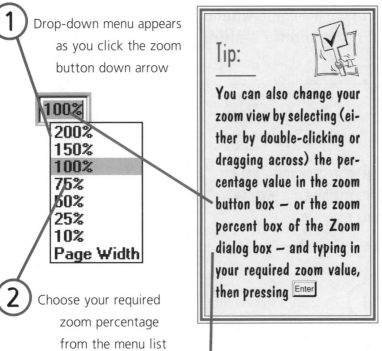

(1) Drop-down menu appears as you click the zoom button down arrow

100%
200%
150%
100%
75%
50%
25%
10%
Page Width

(2) Choose your required zoom percentage from the menu list

Tip:

You can also change your zoom view by selecting (either by double-clicking or dragging across) the percentage value in the zoom button box – or the zoom percent box of the Zoom dialog box – and typing in your required zoom value, then pressing Enter

(3) The Zoom dialog box

Choose your zoom percentage here

A preview gives you some idea of text size

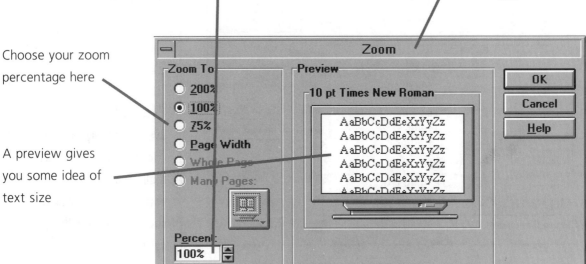

Zoom

Zoom To
○ 200%
◉ 100%
○ 75%
○ Page Width
○ Whole Page
○ Many Pages:

Preview
10 pt Times New Roman
AaBbCcDdEeXxYyZz
AaBbCcDdEeXxYyZz
AaBbCcDdEeXxYyZz
AaBbCcDdEeXxYyZz
AaBbCcDdEeXxYyZz
AaBbCcDdEeXxYyZz

OK
Cancel
Help

Percent:
100%

Saving a document

Once you've worked on a document you need to save it onto disk:

● the document remains in computer memory only as long as Word is running

● if you quit Word, or turn off your machine without saving the document to disk it is lost forever — **RIP**

Take note:

Save your document regularly, throughout working on it. That way, if your machine buckaroos – or you do something silly – your work is not lost – at least upto the last save operation

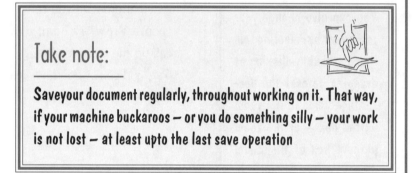

Enter a document name here, or use the suggested default ②

① The Save As dialog box

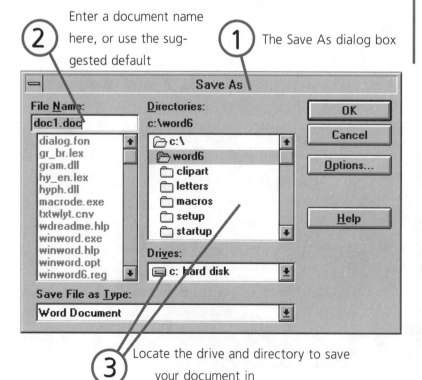

Save As

File **N**ame:
doc1.doc

Directories:
c:\word6

dialog.fon
gr_br.lex
gram.dll
hy_en.lex
hyph.dll
macrode.exe
txtwlyt.cnv
wdreadme.hlp
winword.exe
winword.hlp
winword.opt
winword6.reg

🖿 c:\
📂 word6
📁 clipart
📁 letters
📁 macros
📁 setup
📁 startup

OK
Cancel
Options...
Help

Dri**v**es:
🖴 c: hard disk

Save File as **T**ype:
Word Document

③ Locate the drive and directory to save your document in

Basic steps:

1 Choose **File→Save**, or type [Alt]+[F] then [S], or type [Ctrl]+[S], or click the Save button [🖫]. This calls up the Save As dialog box

2 If this is the first time you have saved the document you should enter a name in the File Name box. If you have already saved the document the Save As dialog box isn't even called up — the document is simply saved over itself with the same file name

3 Locate the drive and directory you want to save the document in, then click OK to save the document

Tip

Yes, we know you haven't even typed anything into a document yet – but saving a document is of *such* importance that we need to cover it now. Use this page as reference!

Opening documents

When you first startup Word a new document is created automatically for you, ready for you to enter text. There are other times, however, when you need to create another new document, or open existing documents you have previously saved.

1 Choose **File⁓Open**, or type [Alt]+[F] then [O], or type [Ctrl]+[O], or click the Open button 🖼. The Open dialog box is shown

2 Locate the document you wish to open in its drive and directory

3 Click OK

(1) The Open dialog box

(3) Click to open the document

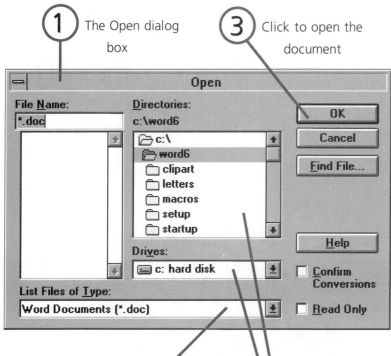

If the document you want to open isn't a Word document with the *.doc* extension, (2) this drop-down box lets you see other openable document types

Locate the document to open in the drive and directory it is saved

File	
New...	Ctrl+N
Open...	Ctrl+O
Close	
Save	Ctrl+S
Save As...	
Save All	
Find File...	
Summary Info...	
Templates...	
Page Setup...	
Print Preview	
Print...	Ctrl+P
1 A:\README.DOC	
2 C:\ST\README.DOC	
Exit	

Tip:

In the File menu is a list of the most recently used documents you've worked on. You can open any document in the list simply by choosing it from the menu

Creating a new document

Creating a new document is just as easy as opening an existing document. Word gives you the option to create the document as the image of a template. Templates are ready-built and installed document *plans*, complete with styles and formats you might want to use for any particular appearance of document (see page 136 for further details of templates).

(see page 136 for further details of templates).

Basic steps:

CREATING NEW DOCUMENTS

1 Choose **File→New**, or type [Alt]+[F] then [N], or type [Ctrl]+[N], ot click the New button [🗋]. The New dialog box is called up

2 Select a template you want your document to follow from the list box

3 Click OK

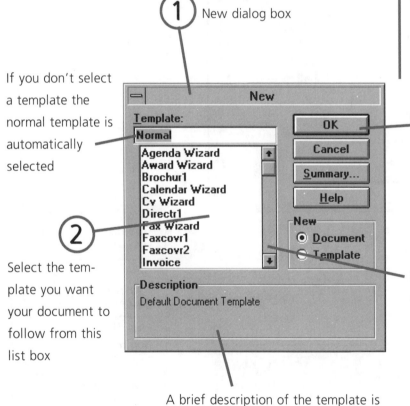

(1) New dialog box

If you don't select a template the normal template is automatically selected

(2) Select the template you want your document to follow from this list box

(3) Click to create a new document with the selected template

Scroll down the list box to see all the available templates

A brief description of the template is displayed here

18

Exiting

After you've finished using a computer program it's usual to exit or quit it. If you're only trying to clear the screen for a short while, on the other hand, there are alternatives.

① The Save Changes? dialog box

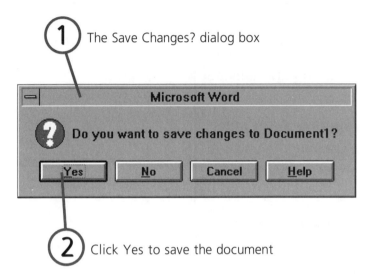

② Click Yes to save the document

1 Choose **File**→**Exit**, or type Alt + F then X. If you have recently saved the document or documents you are working on and have not worked on them since, Word quits straightaway. If you have worked on a document since last saving it (or have not saved it at all) the Save Changes? dialog box is displayed.

2 If you click Yes, Word calls up the Save As dialog box, as on page 16.

Take note:

If you're only trying to clear your screen for a short while — and you don't want to quit Word — click the Minimize button at the top-right of the Word document window. This simply minimizes the window as an icon, left at the bottom of your computer desktop — showing the document name as well as its creator (Word).

To maximize the document (and Word) once again on the screen, simply double-click the icon.

Summary for Section 1

● Startup Word by double-clicking its icon in Program Manager.

● Get on-line help by double-clicking the Help button 【▶?】 in the standard toolbar. Then select the topic you want help on.

● Get faster on-line help by single-clicking the Help button 【▶?】, then click on the button, object, or menu command you want help on.

● Access toolbars by either clicking on any toolbar with the right mouse button then selecting the one you want, or choose **View↪Toolbars** to call up the Toolbars dialog box.

● Change document view between normal, page layout and outline to suit the way you work.

● Page layout view lets you see the page as it will be printed.

● Outline view lets you rearrange headings and their hierarchies, as well as dragging text large distances easily in the document.

● Remove all on-screen clutter with full screen view by choosing **View↪Full Screen**

● Open existing Word documents — or other applications' documents — from the Open dialog box.

● Create a new document — in the form of a selected template — in the New dialog box.

2   Text essentials

Entering text

As a word processor, of course, Word's main function is to store straightforward text. As you startup Word, or create a new document, you can begin to enter text immediately.

Basic steps:

1 Simply type something. It doesn't matter what — a few lines of rubbish will do nicely

2 If the document is important, remember to save it

(1) Enter text into document

(2) Click the save button to save your document

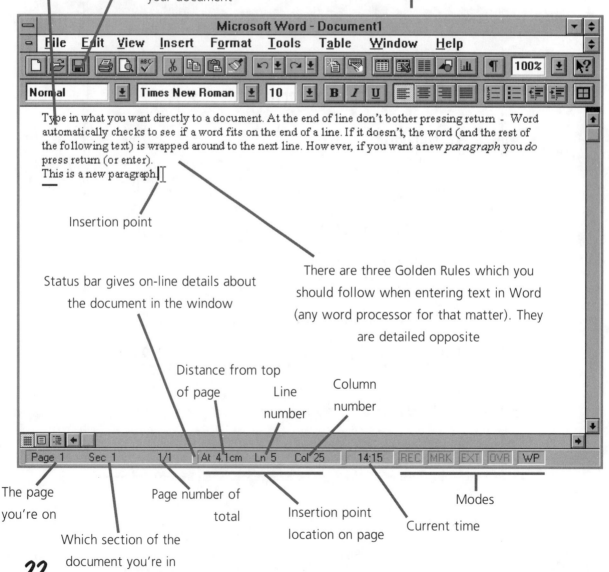

Type in what you want directly to a document. At the end of line don't bother pressing return - Word automatically checks to see if a word fits on the end of a line. If it doesn't, the word (and the rest of the following text) is wrapped around to the next line. However, if you want a new *paragraph* you *do* press return (or enter).
This is a new paragraph.

Insertion point

Status bar gives on-line details about the document in the window

There are three Golden Rules which you should follow when entering text in Word (any word processor for that matter). They are detailed opposite

Distance from top of page

Line number

Column number

| Page 1 | Sec 1 | 1/1 | At 4.1cm | Ln 5 | Col 25 | 14:15 | REC | MRK | EXT | OVR | WP |

The page you're on

Page number of total

Insertion point location on page

Modes

Current time

Which section of the document you're in

22

The status bar

Get into the habit of looking at the status bar. It gives some explicit information about what's happening within your Word document, such as:

❏ page number, section (you can break your document up into smaller sections, to make it more manageable — see page 72) number, and total number of pages

❏ location of the insertion point (that is, the point within text where your keyboard entries appear on screen)

❏ current time (saves you having to waste working time looking up at the clock on the wall!)

❏ mode buttons — accessed by double-clicking — of these only two are of importance here, and are:

❏ WP — on-line help for ex-WordPerfect users. See over for details

❏ OVR — active when blacked (that is, not greyed). See over for details

Take note:

The Golden Rules of Word

1 Never, never, never, never, never, never, never, never, never, never (get the message?) put two spaces together. The old typists' routine of putting two spaces at the end of a sentence should not be done in a word processor because spaces aren't generally of a fixed width. A program like Word adjusts spaces to ensure the text fits its given column width and looks good. Two or more spaces together may be adjusted in width to give ridiculously wide spaces between words. For the same reason, text which is formed into tabular columns mustn't be created by inserting spaces to line columns up — it might look aligned on screen, but when it prints you can't guarantee it — use proper tabs instead (see page 54)

2 Never, never, never, never (oh, here we go again) put two carriage returns together. Actually, this isn't quite so critical as Golden Rule number 1, but important nevertheless. Spaces between paragraphs are best controlled by creating styles for each paragraph type (see section 6) which incorporate spaces before and after them

3 Never (once is enough this time, I'm sure) press ⏎ or Enter at the end of a line of text — unless the end of the line is also the end of a paragraph. There is simply no need — and carriage returns fix the text to those line lengths. Use Word's word-wrapping facility to do it automatically — then any textual style changes will automatically create consequent new word-wraps, too

Help – I'm not-so perfect

If you've previously used WordPerfect as your word processor, then some of Word's features will probably be confusing to you. Help is at hand in the form of a system which correlates specific WordPerfect commands to Word commands.

Basic steps:

1. Type Alt+H, then W, or choose **Help→Word Perfect Help** — or more quickly — double-click the WordPerfect help button WP on the status bar. This calls up the Help for WordPerfect Users dialog box
2. Select the WordPerfect command name in the command keys box
3. Read the information about the command
4. For a demonstration of the command, click Demo

1 The Help for WordPerfect Users dialog box

2 Select the WordPerfect command you are familar with here

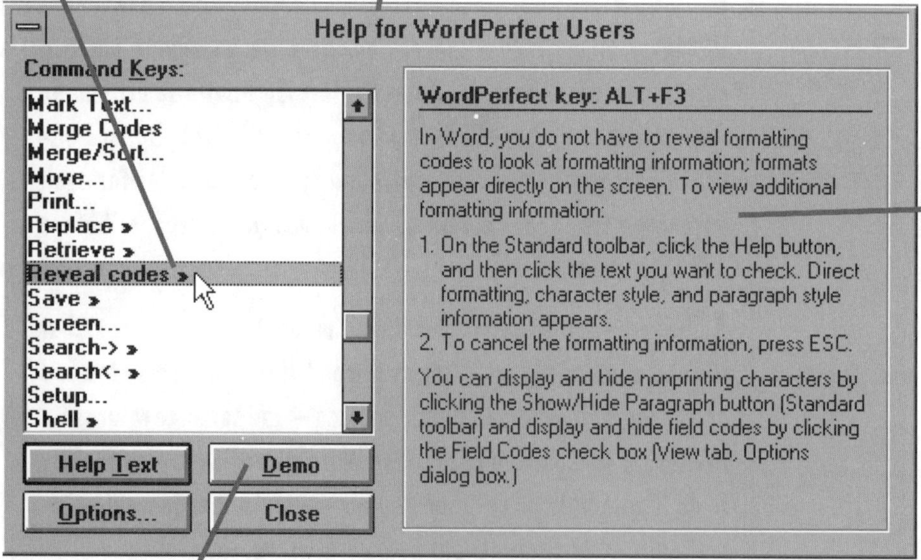
Help for WordPerfect Users
Command Keys:
Mark Text...
Merge Codes
Merge/Sort...
Move...
Print...
Replace »
Retrieve »
Reveal codes »
Save »
Screen...
Search-> »
Search<- »
Setup...
Shell »
Help Text
Demo
Options...
Close
WordPerfect key: ALT+F3
In Word, you do not have to reveal formatting codes to look at formatting information; formats appear directly on the screen. To view additional formatting information:
1. On the Standard toolbar, click the Help button, and then click the text you want to check. Direct formatting, character style, and paragraph style information appears.
2. To cancel the formatting information, press ESC.
You can display and hide nonprinting characters by clicking the Show/Hide Paragraph button (Standard toolbar) and display and hide field codes by clicking the Field Codes check box (View tab, Options dialog box.)

3 Read information about your selected command

4 Click for a demonstration

Editing text

Inevitably you will make mistakes in your work. This is where a word processor like Word shows its forté. On a typewriter, mistakes have to be erased and re-typed, usually resulting in a shoddy document. In a word processor, on the other hand, mistakes are simply edited on-screen before printing. Even if a mistake slips by you, and you only see it after printing, you can correct it and re-print the document.

Even if your required corrections aren't due to mistakes, but are straightforward editorial changes, Word has some unbeaten facilities for making any kind of textual change necessary in a document.

There are several ways you can edit text. The simplest — covered on this page — is overtyping. *All* editing procedures, on the other hand, rely on the principle of placing the insertion point at the point which requires editing!

As you move the mouse pointer over text it changes to the I-beam pointer I. When you position the pointer over the point to edit then click, the insertion point of Word becomes active at that point. This whole process of pointing and clicking with the I-beam pointer I is known as *positioning the insertion point*.

Remember it — because all editing relies on it!

①

There was a cow stupefied on a hill. If it hasn't gonn it will be their still. Now is the time for all good men to come to the aid of the party

④ Once overtyping is complete, return to insertion mode

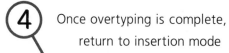

There was a cow stood on a hill. If it hasn't gone it will be there still. Now is the time for all good men to come to the aid of the party I

1 If you spot a mistake which requires you to re-type part or all of a word or sentence, position the insertion point at the beginning of the mistake

2 Double-click the overtype button `OVR` on the status bar to enter overtype mode

3 Re-type the section of text — this overtypes text already there

4 Move to any other areas you need to overtype as in Step 1

5 When you have finished overtyping double-click the overtype button `OVR` again, to return to insertion mode

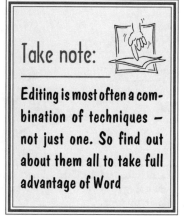

Take note:

Editing is most often a combination of techniques — not just one. So find out about them all to take full advantage of Word

Selecting text

Whenever you want to edit text (that is, apart from when you overtype — see previous page) you need to select the particular text you want to change:

● Word allows you to do this in various ways

● no single way is best

● instead, a combination of selecting techniques — depending on what is to be selected — should be used

● selection of text is sometimes known by different names such as blocking or highlighting. These names are often merely descriptive of the selection process — text which is selected becomes highlighted or blocked and that's how you know the text happens to be selected!

1 You can select any letter, word, sentence, paragraph, or any part of these by dragging over the required text

2 To select a single word, double-click the word

3 To select more than one word, drag from one word across to the next, or further if you want more words to be selected

4 To select a whole line of text, click in the selection bar to the left of the line

Drag the I-beam pointer I over the letters, or words, or sentences, or paragraphs you want to be selected

(1)

No, no, no, said the Giant. There can be no suggestion of a compromise. I am going to eat you all up, because that's the sort of thing giants are known to do.

As you drag over your selected text and release the mouse button, the selected text becomes highlighted.

Highlighted text is simply the visible sign that the text is selected

You can select a single word most quickly by double-clicking the word

(2)

No, no, no, said the Giant. There can be no suggestion of a compromise. I am going to eat you all up, because that's the sort of thing giants are known to do.

Drag over words to select them. As you drag over
each new part of a word the whole word
becomes selected automatically

(3)

No, no, no, said the Giant. There can be no suggsetion of a compromise.
I am going to eat you all up, because that's the sort of thing giants are
known to do.

Tip:

When you begin selecting in the middle of a word, then drag to
include part of another word, Word automatically selects both
words (and any susequent ones too) and any space after the words

Select whole lines of text by clicking in the
selection bar

(4)

The selection bar is to the
left of text on any Word
document page

No, no, no, said the Giant. There can be no suggsetion of a compromise.
I am going to eat you all up, because that's the sort of thing giants are
known to do.

Take note:

All of these selection techniques can be used to select graphic
items, such as pictures, as well as text

Selecting text (contd)

No, no, no, said the Giant. There can be no suggsetion of a compromise. I am going to eat you all up, because that's the sort of thing giants are known to do.

(5) Select multiple lines of text by dragging in the selection bar

Select a single sentence by holding down and clicking in the sentence

(6)

No, no, no, said the Giant. There can be no suggsetion of a compromise. I am going to eat you all up, because that's the sort of thing giants are known to do.

Double-click in the selection bar (or triple-click in the text) to select a paragraph

(7)

No, no, no, said the Giant. There can be no suggsetion of a compromise. I am going to eat you all up, because that's the sort of thing giants are known to do.

Drag across paragraphs in the selection bar to select multiple paragraphs

(8)

No, no, no, said the Giant. There can be no suggsetion of a compromise. I am going to eat you all up, because that's the sort of thing giants are known to do.
With that he picked up Jack and lifted him towards his mouth. Once inside the Giant's mouth Jack realised his time was nigh unless he did some quick thinking. He decided to go for broke and tickled the Giant's tonsils.

5 To select multiple lines of text, drag in the selection bar to the left of the lines

6 To select a sentence, hold down Ctrl and click anywhere in the sentence

7 To select a paragragh, either double-click in the selection bar to the left of the paragraph, or triple-click anywhere in the text

8 To select multiple paragraphs, drag in the selection bar to the left of the paragraphs

9 To select an entire document, triple-click in the selection bar

10 Select text which is neither a whole word, sentence, or paragraph by positioning the insertion point at the beginning of the text, then holding down Shift while you click at the end of the text

Select an entire document's text by triple-clicking in the selection bar

⑨

> Take two aspirins and call me in the mroning. The dogs sat on the mat. When the Queen of Hearts had no tea the Knave of Hearts stole the tarts. Instead she beat the Knave of Hearts soundly and sent him to bed.
>
> No, no, no, said the Giant. There can be no suggsetion of a compromise. I am going to eat you all up, because that's the sort of thing giants are known to do.
>
> With that he picked up Jack and lifted him towards his mouth. Once inside the Giant's mouth Jack realised his time was nigh unless he did some quick thinking. He decided to go for broke and tickled the Giant's tonsils.

Tip: ✓

Cancel a selection by clicking outside of it, or pressing any arrow key

⑩

By clicking at the starting point, then holding down [Shift] and clicking at the finishing point, a complete block of text can be selected

> No, no, no, said the Giant. There can be no suggsetion of a compromise. I am going to eat you all up, because that's the sort of thing giants are known to do.
>
> With that he picked up Jack and lifted him towards his mouth. Once inside the Giant's mouth Jack realised his time was nigh unless he did some quick thinking. He decided to go for broke and tickled the Giant's tonsils.

KEYBOARD SHORTCUTS

You can select text with the keyboard too:

One character right	[Shift] + [→]
One character left	[Shift] + [←]
To the end of a word	[Ctrl] + [Shift] + [→]
To the beginning of a word	[Ctrl] + [Shift] + [←]
To the end of a line	[Shift] + [End]
To the beginning of a line	[Shift] + [Home]
One line down	[Shift] + [↓]
One line up	[Shift] + [↑]
To the end of a paragraph	[Ctrl] + [Shift] + [↓]
To the start of a paragraph	[Ctrl] + [Shift] + [↑]
One screen down	[Shift] + [Page Down]
One screen up	[Shift] + [Page Up]
To end of document	[Ctrl] + [Shift] + [End]
To beginning of document	[Ctrl] + [Shift] + [Home]
Entire document	[Ctrl] + [A]
To a specific location	[F8] +arrow keys

Tip: ✓

Whatever you do in Word – writing, editing, stylising, formatting and so on – relies on being able to select text.

No single selection method is best for all purposes. Depending on what you want to select, you should choose the preferred method. Sometimes you should use the mouse, sometimes you should use the keyboard.

The only way you can make sure you use the preferred method for any particular purpose is to learn how to use all methods

Cut, copy and paste

Word (like any Windows application) uses a temporary storage area known as the Clipboard to keep items you want to move or copy within a Word document. These items can be of text or graphic forms (or a mixture of both). Using the Clipboard to do this is known as cutting, copying and pasting:

● you *cut* an item onto the Clipboard when you want to remove it from one place in a document and move it to another place

● you *copy* an item onto the Clipboard when you want it to occur at more than one place in your document

● taking an item from the Clipboard and putting it in your document is known as *pasting.*

CUTTING

1 Select the item or items you want to cut onto the clipboard. This can be a selection of text, a graphical item, or a combination of the two

2 Choose **Edit↪Cut**, or type `Alt`+`E` then `T`, or type `Ctrl`+`X`, or simply click the Cut button to cut the selected item — it disappears from your Word document and is moved onto the Clipboard

Come and see the show

On the other hand, this is a boring part of this document. Let's liven it up by moving the graphic down here!

(1) & (3)

Select the item or items to be cut or copied

Use whichever selection method is appropriate for the text (or graphic in this case) to be copied or cut. To select this graphic, clicking in the selection bar is fastest

(2) Cut the item or items (now you see it — now you don't!)

Come and see the show

On the other hand, this is a boring part of this document. Let's liven it up by moving the graphic down here!

Position the insertion point before pasting

(5) | I

COPYING

3 Select the item or items you want to copy

4 Choose **Edit↪Copy**, or type ⎡Alt⎤+⎡E⎤ then ⎡C⎤, or type ⎡Ctrl⎤+⎡C⎤, or click the Copy button — the selection stays in your document but is copied onto the Clipboard too

PASTING

5 Position the insertion point where you want the item or items stored on the Clipboard to be pasted

6 Choose **Edit↪Paste**, or type ⎡Alt⎤+⎡E⎤ then ⎡P⎤, or type ⎡Ctrl⎤+⎡V⎤, or click the Paste button to paste the item or items into your document

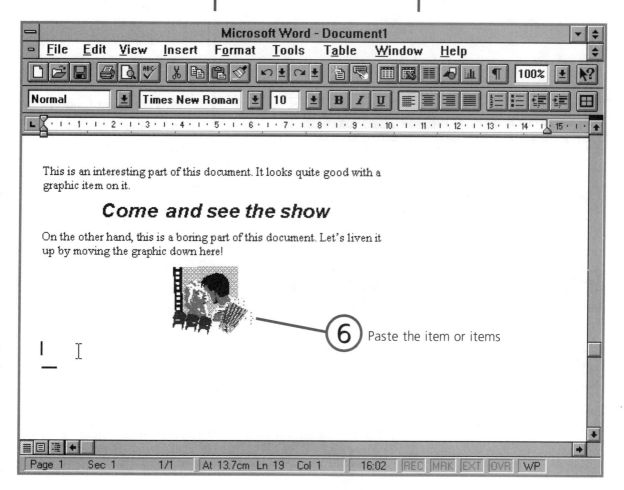

31

Drag-and-drop editing

Word has an extremely useful feature in its ability to allow selected text to be moved or copied by dragging. Proper use of this drag-and-drop editing can speed up incorporation of revisions in a document.

(1) Select the text

> Take two aspirins and call me in the mroning. The dogs sat on the mat. When the Queen of Hearts had no tea the Knave of Hearts stole the tarts. Instead she beat the Knave of Hearts soundly and sent him to bed.

The arrow pointer replaces the I-beam pointer over selected text

(2)

> Take two aspirins and call me in the mroning. The dogs sat on the mat. When the Queen of Hearts had no tea the Knave of Hearts stole the tarts. Instead she beat the Knave of Hearts soundly and sent him to bed.

As you drag the selected text, the drag-and-drop pointer is displayed

(3)

> Take two aspirins and call me in the mroning. The dogs sat on the mat. When the Queen of Hearts had no tea the Knave of Hearts stole the tarts. Instead she beat the Knave of Hearts soundly and sent him to bed.

(4) The dotted insertion point tells you where the text will be moved to

(5) The text moves as you let go the mouse button

> Take two aspirins and call me in the mroning. The dogs sat on the mat. When the Knave of Hearts stole the tarts the Queen of Hearts had no tea. Instead she beat the Knave of Hearts soundly and sent him to bed.

MOVING SELECTED TEXT

1 Select the text to be moved

2 Position the pointer over the selected text (the I-beam pointer I changes to the arrow pointer

3 Click on the selected text and drag the pointer — it changes to the drag-and-drop pointer

4 As you drag the drag-and-drop pointer to a new position, the dotted insertion point follows indicating where the selected text will be dragged to

5 When you have located the dotted insertion point where you want, release the mouse button. The selected text moves to the new location

COPYING SELECTED TEXT

6 Select text as before

7 Drag the selected text as before

8 Locate the position you wish to copy text to as before (with the dotted insertion point)

9 Before you let go the mouse button, press and hold down Ctrl (the drag-and-drop pointer changes to show a plus symbol indicating Word is ready to copy (that is, not just move) text

10 Let go the mouse button. The selected text is copied to the new location

Tip:
_____

Drag-and-drop editing is really just an extension of the cut, copy and paste principle. As a result, you can drag-and-drop graphical items, or a combination of graphical and text items, as well as just text

No, no, no, said the Giant. There can be no suggsetion of a compromise. I am going to eat you all up, because that's the sort of thing giants are known to do

6 Select text to be copied

7 Drag selected text with drag-and-drop pointer

No, no, no, said the Giant. There can be no suggsetion of a compromise. I am going to eat you all up, because that's the sort of thing giants are known to do.

8 Locate the dotted insertion point where you want the text to be copied to

No, no, no, said the Giant. There can be no suggsetion of a compromise. I am going to eat you all up, because that's the sort of thing giants are known to do.

9 Hold down Ctrl to copy selected text (indicated by + symbol on drag-and-drop pointer)

10 As you release the mouse button, selected text is copied

No, no, no, no, no, said the Giant. There can be no suggsetion of a compromise. I am going to eat you all up, because that's the sort of thing giants are known to do.

Oops – a mistake

Word processors are meant to make the correction of mistakes as simple as possible. Apart from the proper editing facilities of Word we've already seen, however, are extra goodies which make the correction of simple typing errors almost as easy as making the mistakes in the first place — but not qwite, if you see what I mean!

It's as well to know all these goodies to get the best out of Word. The mistakes we're concerned with here are those which you notice almost as you make them:

- obvious spelling errors

- mis-hit keys

- style changes which shouldn't have been made

and so on.

1 If you have just a few letters you want to delete, a quick result can be to press [Back space], or [Delete]:

❏ [Back space] deletes the character before the insertion point

❏ [Delete] deletes the character after the insertion point

❏ [Ctrl]+[Back space] deletes the word before the insertion point

❏ [Ctrl]+[Delete] deletes the word after the insertion point

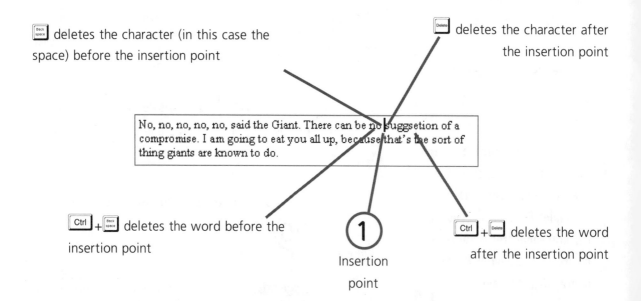

[Back space] deletes the character (in this case the space) before the insertion point

[Delete] deletes the character after the insertion point

No, no, no, no, no, said the Giant. There can be no suggsetion of a compromise. I am going to eat you all up, because that's the sort of thing giants are known to do.

[Ctrl]+[Back space] deletes the word before the insertion point

1
Insertion point

[Ctrl]+[Delete] deletes the word after the insertion point

2 You can very often *undo* a mistake or change you make in a Word document, because Word features a multiple undo facility. Just click the Undo button 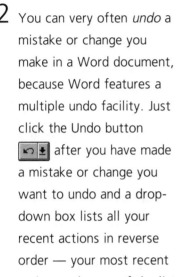 after you have made a mistake or change you want to undo and a drop-down box lists all your recent actions in reverse order — your most recent action at the top of the list

Tip:

Your most recent action can also be undone by choosing **Edit↵Undo**, or typing Alt + E then U, or typing Ctrl + Z

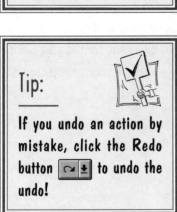

Tip:

If you undo an action by mistake, click the Redo button to undo the undo!

 Take note:

Actions can only be undone in strict order – if you want to undo the action 48 places down the list, the most recent 47 actions have to be undone also!

Clicking the Undo button
(2) displays a drop-down list box

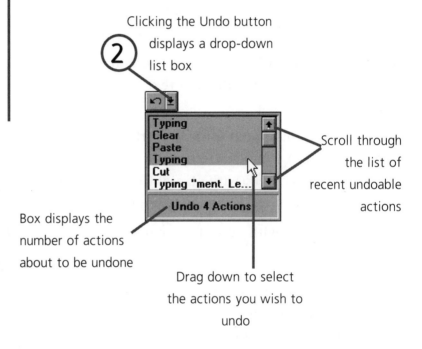

Scroll through the list of recent undoable actions

Box displays the number of actions about to be undone

Drag down to select the actions you wish to undo

Take note:

While Word's undo feature is a boon for those of us who make mistakes – that is, anyone who uses a computer – you should remember that some actions are not undoable

Entering symbols

Although Word is a *word* processor, very often it's necessary to include symbols within text. Examples of such symbols are:

● mathematical or scientific symbols — Ω μ ß Σ for example (however, if you want to include complete mathematical formulae or expressions into your work it is best to use Word's integral equation editor, which is beyond the scope of this book)

● dingbats — the blob or bullet (●) at the left of this list is an example of a dingbat. Others are ✂ ☞ ♣ □ ♠ which can be used to embellish text

● typographical symbols and marks — the most obvious examples of typographical marks are the curly quotes (' and ") which differentiate properly typeset text from typewritten (with straight quotes — ' and ") text together with en dashes (–) and em dashes (—)

● foreign letters with accents — é ü å õ ç

and so on.

The ability to enter such symbols rapidly greatly enhances a word processor. Word has a special Symbol command which simplifies the task.

Tip:

Use typographer's symbols and marks to give your work that professional edge. Automatically include curly quotes using Word's AutoCorrect feature (page 100). Use an en dash to combine number ranges (eg, pages 44–56) and use an em dash to separate emphasising text — just like that!

Basic steps:

1 Position the insertion point where you want the symbol to be (if you are typing in text and want to enter the symbol as you go, the insertion point is already positioned correctly). Now choose **Insert ↳ Symbol**, or type `Alt`+`I` then `S`. This calls up the Symbol dialog box which automatically displays symbols available in the symbol font

2 Click a symbol and it is displayed enlarged. Click Insert if you want the symbol in your text. Alternatively, double-click the symbol you want. It is placed in text at the position of the insertion point

3 Display and choose a different font if you want with the Font drop-down list box

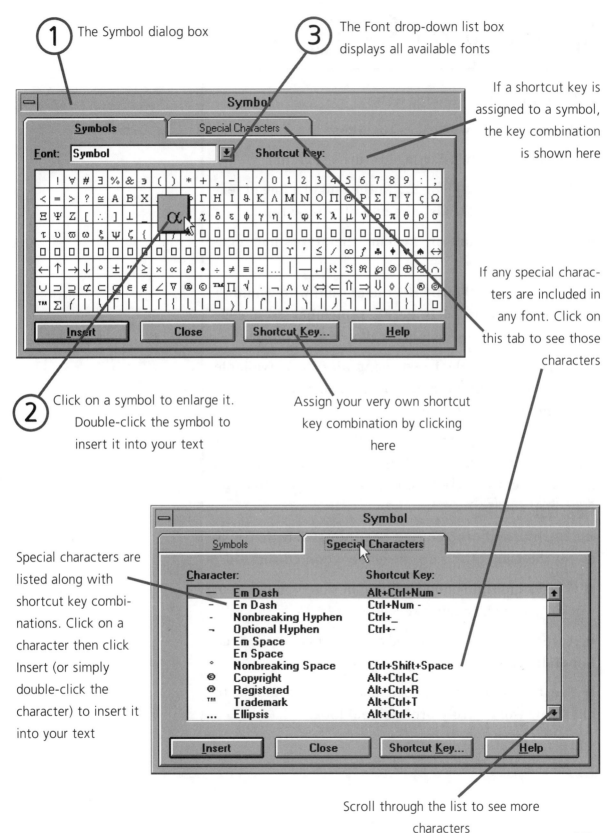

① The Symbol dialog box

③ The Font drop-down list box displays all available fonts

If a shortcut key is assigned to a symbol, the key combination is shown here

If any special characters are included in any font. Click on this tab to see those characters

② Click on a symbol to enlarge it. Double-click the symbol to insert it into your text

Assign your very own shortcut key combination by clicking here

Special characters are listed along with shortcut key combinations. Click on a character then click Insert (or simply double-click the character) to insert it into your text

Scroll through the list to see more characters

37

Summary for Section 2

● Follow the three Golden Rules:

1   never put two spaces together

2   never put two carriage returns together

3   never press ⏎ or Enter at the end of a line of text — unless it is also the end of a paragraph.

● Get into the habit of checking the status bar regularly.

● If you're an ex-WordPerfect user (and who wouldn't be now that Word 6 is here), remember to access Word's on-line help system for WordPerfect users.

● Learn how to select text using *all* of the available methods — no one method is best for all cases, and you really need to know them all.

● Use the cut, copy and paste facility to speed up your work. Learn the keyboard shortcuts (Ctrl+X to cut, Ctrl+C to copy, Ctrl+V to paste), or use the buttons (✂, ⧉, and 📋).

● Use drag-and-drop editing — although a little tricky to get the hang of, it's an extremely good editing aid.

● Word's multiple undo feature can save you hours of work if you make a mistake.

● Access symbols and special characters with the Symbol dialog box.

● Use typographer's special marks and symbols to give your work a truly professional look.

3   Formatting text

About formatting

When you first enter text at the keyboard in Word it is generally unformatted. That is, it is plain, unembellished, with no changes applied to alter its appearance. Generally, it will be in the default font (say, Times New Roman) and a default size (say, 10 point).

Making alterations to text's appearance is known as formatting the text. There are several ways this can be done in Word:

● formatting can be applied by the user to individual or grouped characters — this is known as *character formatting*

● formatting can be applied by the user to whole paragraphs — called (fancy that) *paragraph formatting*

● formatting can be applied automatically by Word — either as you enter text or afterwards, and either across a whole document (using Word's *AutoFormat* feature), or to paragraphs (using *paragraph styles*).

While character and paragraph formatting are both very powerful tools and can give you the visual effects you might require in a document, the *real* power of a word processor like Word lies in its ability to apply automatic formatting.

Take note:

Use character and paragraph formatting by all means – and they're going to be described over the next few pages so you can get to grips with them – but bear in mind that only when you use them to build *automatic* formatting features do they *really* become useful

40

You can format whole lines

You can format individual characters or words

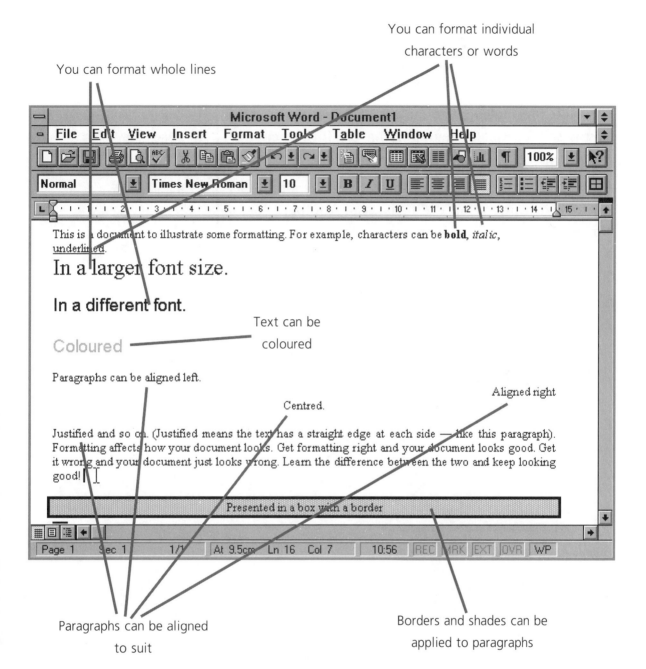

Microsoft Word - Document1

File   Edit   View   Insert   Format   Tools   Table   Window   Help

Normal   Times New Roman   10   **B** *I* U

This is a document to illustrate some formatting. For example, characters can be **bold**, *italic*, underlined.

In a larger font size.

In a different font.

Text can be coloured

Coloured

Paragraphs can be aligned left.

Centred.

Aligned right

Justified and so on. (Justified means the text has a straight edge at each side —like this paragraph). Formatting affects how your document looks. Get formatting right and your document looks good. Get it wrong and your document just looks wrong. Learn the difference between the two and keep looking good!

Presented in a box with a border

Page 1   Sec 1   1/1   At 9.5cm   Ln 16   Col 7   10:56   REC   MRK   EXT   OVR   WP

Paragraphs can be aligned to suit

Borders and shades can be applied to paragraphs

Character formats

Character formatting is a matter of selecting the text you wish to format, then applying the format change you want.

Many of the most common formats are available as buttons or options on the formatting toolbar. Some, however, are accessed by menu choice.

 Select the text to be formatted — this can be an individual letter, a word, group of words, sentence, paragraph, or even the whole document

This is a sample of text in Times New Roman font at 10 point. It will be used to illustrate character formatting.

 Format the selected text to suit — this example shows the selected text emboldened

This is a sample of text in Times New Roman font at 10 point. It will be used to **illustrate character formatting**.

Text you format is displayed formatted on screen. There are no formatting codes (as in some — let's say — lesser-capable word processors). What-you-see on-screen is more-or-less what-you-get on printout

Tip:

To format a single word you don't need to select the word in the usual manner — all you have to do is click anywhere in the word, then apply the format changes you want

There are three main ways you can apply formatting to text:

1 From the formatting toolbar — buttons or options

The formatting toolbar gives the easiest options to change common formats ①

Click buttons to apply (or re-move) bold, italic, and underline

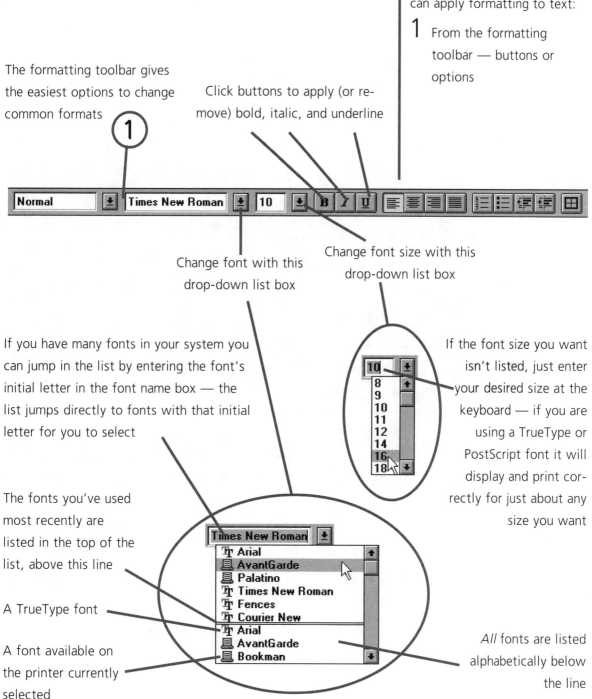

| Normal | ± | Times New Roman | ± | 10 | ± | B | I | U | ...

Change font with this drop-down list box

Change font size with this drop-down list box

If you have many fonts in your system you can jump in the list by entering the font's initial letter in the font name box — the list jumps directly to fonts with that initial letter for you to select

If the font size you want isn't listed, just enter your desired size at the keyboard — if you are using a TrueType or PostScript font it will display and print cor-rectly for just about any size you want

The fonts you've used most recently are listed in the top of the list, above this line

A TrueType font

A font available on the printer currently selected

All fonts are listed alphabetically below the line

43

Character formats (contd)

Basic steps:

2 From the Font dialog box (choose **Format→Font**, or type [Alt]+[O] then [F] to display it)

The Font dialog box gives some more formatting options (2)

Click this tab to see more options regarding letter spacing and vertical positioning

List box for font size

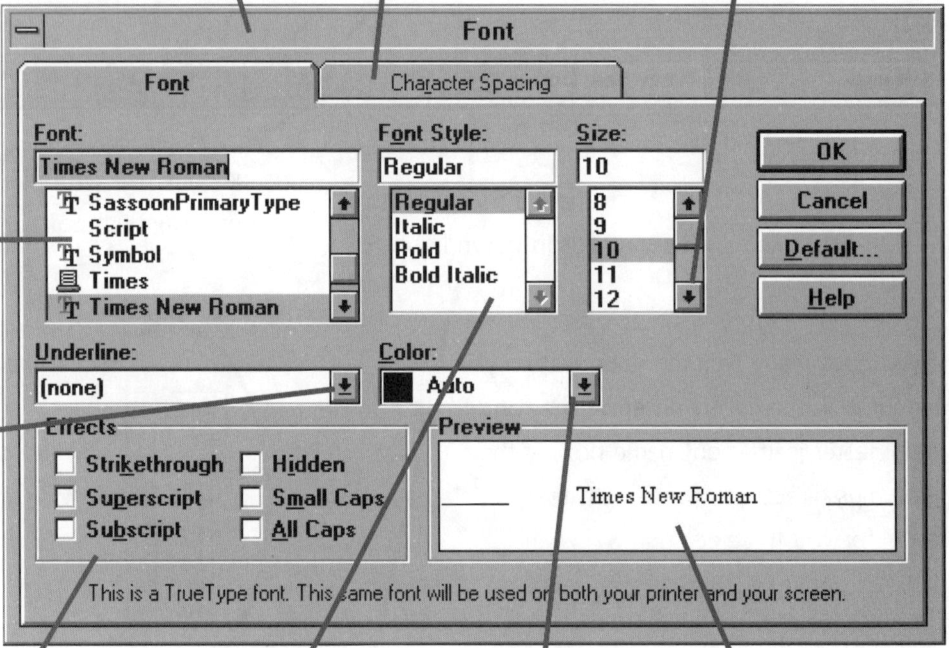

Font
Font
Character Spacing
Font:
Times New Roman
SassoonPrimaryType
Script
Symbol
Times
Times New Roman
Font Style:
Regular
Regular
Italic
Bold
Bold Italic
Size:
10
8
9
10
11
12
OK
Cancel
Default...
Help
Underline:
(none)
Color:
Auto
Effects
Strikethrough
Superscript
Subscript
Hidden
Small Caps
All Caps
Preview
Times New Roman
This is a TrueType font. This same font will be used on both your printer and your screen.

List box for available fonts

Drop-down list box for special underlining effects

Check box options for various formats

List box of bold and italic format options

Drop-down list box holding available colours to format text with

Preview box, to see the effects of formats you have selected

3 With keyboard combinations. These can very often provide the quickest methods of applying formats

KEYBOARD SHORTCUT COMBINATIONS

Many formatting options can best be applied with a keyboard shortcut:

Bold	`Ctrl` + `B`
Italic	`Ctrl` + `I`
Underline	`Ctrl` + `U`
Word underline	`Ctrl` + `Shift` + `W`
Double underline	`Ctrl` + `Shift` + `D`
Subscript	`Ctrl` + `=`
Superscript	`Ctrl` + `Shift` + `=`
Small caps	`Ctrl` + `Shift` + `K`
All caps	`Ctrl` + `Shift` + `A`
Change case	`Shift` + `F3`
Hidden text	`Ctrl` + `Shift` + `H`
Copy formats	`Ctrl` + `Shift` + `C`
Paste formats	`Ctrl` + `Shift` + `V`
Remove formats	`Ctrl` +SPACEBAR
Font	`Ctrl` + `Shift` + `F`
Symbol font	`Ctrl` + `Shift` + `Q`
Point size	`Ctrl` + `Shift` + `P`
next up	`Ctrl` + `>`
next down	`Ctrl` + `<`
up one point	`Ctrl` + `]`
down one point	`Ctrl` + `[`

Tip:

You can apply a format to the insertion point too. This way, anything you type after the format is applied has that format, until you change it again. This is useful for, say, italicising a single word for emphasis as you type it – just apply the italic format before you type the word, then remove the italic format (hence returning to regular text) after the word is finished

Character formats (contd)

There's a few points worth remembering about character formatting in Word. These are shown here as tips for you to use as reference.

Tip:

Your last formatting action can be repeated by choosing Edit⇥Repeat Formatting, or typing [Alt]+[E] then [R], or typing [Ctrl]+[Y].

Note that all formats applied via the Font dialog box will be re-applied as one, whereas only the last individual formatting action applied with, say, buttons on the Formatting toolbar is re-applied

Tip:

Removing a character format follows the same procedure as applying it in the first place. You first select the character, characters, word, words, sentence, paragraph and so on, then you go through the same steps you took to originally apply it. If a word is emboldened, for example, you simply select it then click the Bold button [B] on the formatting toolbar to remove the format

Tip:

You can remove *all* formatting applied by the methods shown over these last few pages to text, by first selecting the text then typing

[Ctrl]+SPACEBAR.

Note, though, that this does not remove formatting applied as part of styles (see page 118)

Painting a format

If you see text which is formatted the way you want another selection of text to be formatted, you can copy the formatting onto further text with the Format Painter button on the Standard toolbar.

①　Select the text with the format you want to copy (in this case an italicised word)

> Take it from me. There's no *point* in trying to pass your driving test. Within ten years at most — more likely five — there'll be so many cars on the road that no-one will be able to drive more than 35 miles per hour anyway. And where's the fun in that?

③　Select the text to be formatted

> Take it from me. There's no *point* in trying to pass your driving test. Within ten years at most — more likely five — there'll be so many cars on the road that no-one will be able to drive more than 35 miles hour anyway. And where's the fun in that?

Once selected, the text is automatically formatted

> Take it from me. There's no *point* in trying to pass your driving test. Within ten years at most — more likely five — there'll be so many cars on the road that no-one will be able to *drive more than 35 miles per* hour anyway. And where's the fun in that?

1 Select the text, part of text, or simply position the insertion point anywhere inside the text you wish to copy the formatting from

2 Click the Format Painter button on the Standard toolbar. The pointer changes to the format painter pointer

3 Select the text you want to be formatted with that format

✔ Tip:

If you double-click the Format Painter button after selecting text with the format you want to copy, the format painter pointer remains active after you have painted the format to further text. You can continue to paint the format for as long as you want onto more selections of text. Click the Format Painter button again to de-activate the format painter pointer

✔ Tip:

You don't even need to select a single word if you want to paint another word's format onto it with the format painter pointer. Just click anywhere inside the word and the format is painted over the whole word

47

Paragraph formats

Whereas character formats affect just the *characters* you select, paragraph formats control the — you've got it — *paragraphs.* In other words, complete blocks of text and their line spacings, indents or alignments for example, are affected by paragraph formats. Paragraph formats *do not just affect* single characters, words, or sentences.

Paragraph marks (¶) indicate where a paragraph ends

Note that while all these paragraphs in this screenshot of a Word document have the same character formats (they are all in the same font, size, and so on) they still *appear* different, because their paragraph formats are differents

This·is·a·left-aligned·paragraph.¶

This·is·a·right-aligned·paragraph.¶

This·is·a·centred·paragraph.¶

This·paragraph·has·single·line-spacing·and·is·indented·by·a· small·amount·on·its·first·line.·Lines·are·close·together,·set·by· Word·itself.·This·is·a·standard·setting·unless·you·change·the· default·style·(covered·later·in·the·book).¶

This·paragraph·has·double·line-spacing·and·is·indented·

on·its·first·line·by·a·slightly·larger·amount.·Lines·are·obviously·

wider·apart·than·the·previous·paragraph.·It's·possible·to·do·this·

all·in·Word·quite·simply·when·you·know·what·you're·doing.¶

Paragraph marks (¶) are used by Word to store a paragraph's formatting

Take note:

A paragraph is defined as any block of text – no matter how short, or how long – ending with a paragraph mark ¶. A paragraph mark is added to your text each time you press Enter or ⏎.

Paragraph marks *may* be hidden – to display them (or hide them if they are currently displayed) click the Show/Hide ¶ button ¶ on the Standard toolbar

To apply a paragraph format to a paragraph you use the same techniques you use to apply a character format to a character.

1 Select the paragraph or paragraphs (in this example there are two paragraphs) you want to format

Here·we·go,·here·we·go,·here·we·go.·It's·another·fine,·fine·day· down·at·the·ranch.··The·brunch·is·cooking·and·the·horses·are· lively.··After·we've·eaten·we'll·get·going·and·round-up·the·cattle.· Never·in·the·field·of·human·conflict·has·so·much·been·eaten·by· so·few.¶
Inevitably,·there·will·be·a·cut·in·resources.··There's·now·so·little· money·to·go·round·that·it's·just·a·question·of·jobs·or·the·tools·to· do·those·jobs.·If·we·want·to·maintain·current·levels·of· employment,·we'll·all·just·have·to·do·with·less·to·spend.¶

Take note:

You don't have to select a whole paragraph before you apply paragraph formatting to it. If you position the insertion point *anywhere* within the paragraph then apply paragraph formatting the *entire* paragraph is formatted

Tip:

If you are currently typing text into a formatted paragraph, then press Enter or ⏎, the new paragraph so created continues with the format of the preceding paragraph. In other words, if you have formatted a paragraph to the paragraph style you want, each subsequent paragraph has the same format

Apply the paragraph formats — here the paragraphs have been indented on their first lines and justified **2**

       Here·we·go,·here·we·go,·here·we·go.·It's·another· fine,·fine·day·down·at·the·ranch.··The·brunch·is·cooking·and·the· horses·are·lively.·After·we've·eaten·we'll·get·going·and·round-up· the·cattle.·Never·in·the·field·of·human·conflict·has·so·much·been· eaten·by·so·few.¶
       Inevitably,·there·will·be·a·cut·in·resources.··There's· now·so·little·money·to·go·round·that·it's·just·a·question·of·jobs·or· the·tools·to·do·those·jobs.··If·we·want·to·maintain·current·levels· of·employment,·we'll·all·just·have·to·do·with·less·to·spend.¶

Paragraph formats (contd)

Like character formats, paragraph formats can be applied to text in three main ways.

1 Paragraph formats can be applied from the Formatting toolbar (some are applied from the ruler, too)

The Formatting toolbar, shown with the ruler

Centre align button

Justify button

Button to increase indent from the left margin

Left align button

Right align button

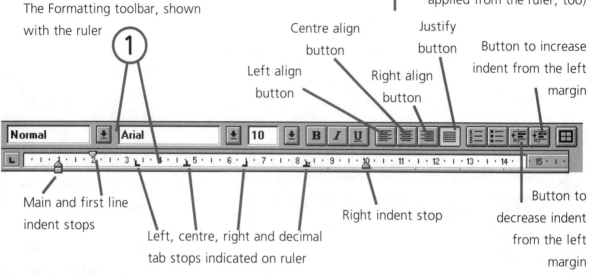

Main and first line indent stops

Left, centre, right and decimal tab stops indicated on ruler

Right indent stop

Button to decrease indent from the left margin

Tip:

Unlike some word processors, Word does not use formatting codes. The formats you apply are visible directly on-screen, so you can see what they will print like. If, however, you want to see the particular

paragraph (or character) formats applied, click the Help button **[\?]** on the Standard toolbar, then click in the paragraph.

A Paragraph Formatting dialog box is displayed which shows the formatting applied. Click the Help button **[\?]** again, or press **[Esc]** to get rid of it

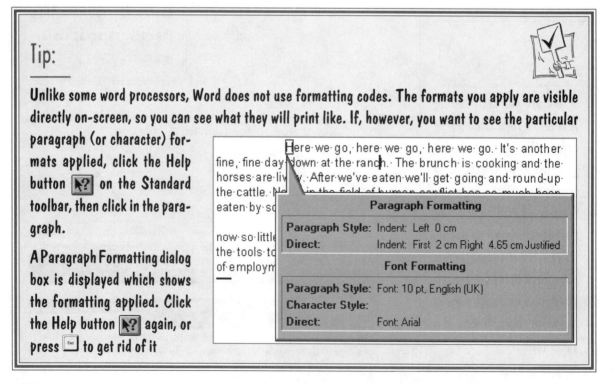

2 Formats can be applied from the Paragraph dialog box (to display it choose **Format⌐→Paragraph**, or type `Alt`+`O` then `P`)

2 The Paragraph dialog box, from which many paragraph formatting options can be set as one step

Click this tab for special text flow options (see over)

Special indenting options drop-down list box

Preview of how formats affect your selected paragraph

See tip below

Line spacing drop-down list box

Alignment drop-down list box

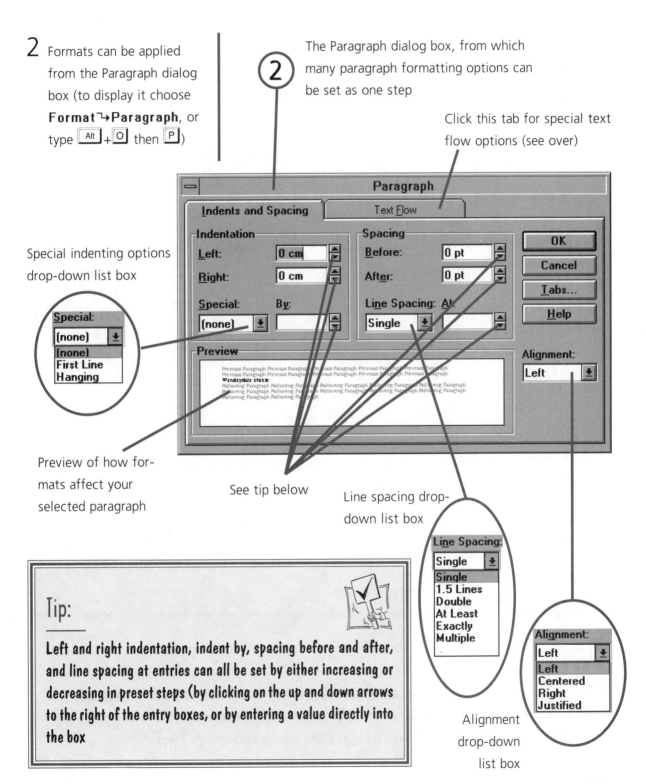

Tip:

Left and right indentation, indent by, spacing before and after, and line spacing at entries can all be set by either increasing or decreasing in preset steps (by clicking on the up and down arrows to the right of the entry boxes, or by entering a value directly into the box

Paragraph formats (contd)

Special paragraph formatting attributes are available from the Text Flow tab option of the Paragraph dialog box. These attributes affect the way text flows between pages of a document. Main ones are labelled and described.

Checking this check box prevents the last line of a paragraph from being printed at the top of a page (a widow), or the first line of a paragraph from being printed alone at the bottom of a page (an orphan)

Checking this prevents a paragraph from being split from the following paragraph

Checking this prevents a paragraph being split across pages at all

Checking this inserts a page break before a paragraph (in other words, the paragraph will be at the top of a new page)

Paragraph

Indents and Spacing | Text Flow

Pagination

- ☒ Widow/Orphan Control
- ☐ Keep Lines Together
- ☑ Keep with Next
- ☐ Page Break Before

- ☐ Suppress Line Numbers
- ☐ Don't Hyphenate

OK
Cancel
Tabs...
Help

Preview

Previous Paragraph Previous Paragraph Previous Paragraph Previous Paragraph Previous Paragraph
Previous Paragraph Previous Paragraph Previous Paragraph Previous Paragraph Previous Paragraph
Sample Text Sample Text Sample Text Sample Text Sample Text Sample Text Sample Text Sample
Text Sample Text Sample Text Sample Text Sample Text Sample Text Sample Text Sample Text
Sample Text Sample Text Sample Text Sample Text Sample Text Sample Text
Following Paragraph Following Paragraph Following Paragraph Following Paragraph Following Paragraph
Following Paragraph Following Paragraph Following Paragraph Following Paragraph Following Paragraph
Following Paragraph Following Paragraph

Tip:

These attributes can make a document look much better and prevent anomalies. If the Keep with Next option is checked for a paragraph formatted as a heading which by chance falls at the bottom of a page, for example, it will be forced onto the next page along with its accompanying text

Basic steps:

3 Paragraph formats can be applied directly with keyboard shortcut combinations. Like character formatting keyboard combinations, these are very often the quickest ways of applying certain formats.

KEYBOARD SHORTCUT COMBINATIONS

Left-align text	Ctrl + B
Centre align text	Ctrl + E
Right-align text	Ctrl + R
Justify text	Ctrl + J
Indent from left margin	Ctrl + M
Decrease indent	Ctrl + Shift + M
Create a hanging indent	Ctrl + T
Decrease a hanging indent	Ctrl + Shift + T
1 line space	Ctrl + 1
1.5 line space	Ctrl + 5
2 line space	Ctrl + 2
Add or remove 12 points of space before a paragraph	Ctrl + 0
Remove paragraph formats not applied by a style	Ctrl + Q
Restore Normal style	Ctrl + Shift + N
Display or hide nonprinting characters (¶ and so on)	Ctrl + *

Tip:

You can most quickly indent selected paragraphs using either the keyboard shortcut combinations above right, or (even better) using the Decrease Indent or Increase Indent buttons on the Formatting toolbar.

While changes due to either of these methods are in fixed increments you can always later change them by dragging indent markers on the ruler

Take note:

While character and paragraph formats are all very nice, and very good, and used properly can greatly improve the look of a document, bear in mind you have to apply every one of them individually.

On the other hand, you can apply formats automatically by using styles (page 118) and Word's AutoFormat command (page 132). Automatic formatting is much quicker and, because you can use both methods across documents, ensures that documents you create can have a unified style, or set of styles, giving a much more professional appearance to your work

Tabs

As a typewriter, any word processor has the ability to define tab stops. These are used to help align text, such that tables or columns of figures, say, can be neatened up and aligned underneath each other.

Better than a typewriter, on the other hand, word processors usually have more than just one type of tab stop. Where typewriters only align text so that text is left-aligned after the tab stop, Word allows text to be:

● left-aligned — as on a typewriter, with text aligned after the tab stop

● centre-aligned — with text centred around the tab stop

● right-aligned — where text is aligned-right to the tab stop

● decimal-aligned — with monetary figures, say, aligned so their decimal point is aligned directly on the tab stop

● bar-aligned — Word creates a vertical line in your document, the height of the text line, at the tab stop.

Tip

You move to a tab stop when you're typing simply by pressing . This action moves the insertion point to the next tab stop, after which you can carry on typing. Note (see illustration below) that a character ○ indicates a tab entry in text. These are special characters which are not printed (like paragraph marks ¶) and can be hidden or displayed (just like paragraph marks) by clicking the Show/Hide ¶ button on the Standard toolbar

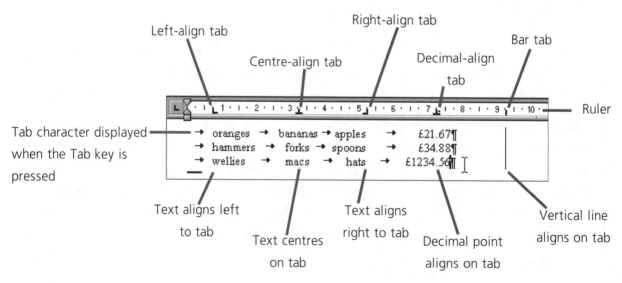

Left-align tab

Centre-align tab

Right-align tab

Decimal-align tab

Bar tab

Ruler

Tab character displayed when the Tab key is pressed

| → | oranges | → | bananas → apples | → | £21.67¶ |

Text aligns left to tab

Text centres on tab

Text aligns right to tab

Decimal point aligns on tab

Vertical line aligns on tab

Basic steps:

The most straightforward way of setting tabs is with the ruler:

1 Repeatedly click the Tab Alignment button (preset as ▣) until the type of tab you require is displayed

▣ — align left

▣ — align centre

▣ — align right

▣ — align to decimal point

2 Click in the ruler at the position you want the tab stop. It is displayed in the ruler as a symbol (according to which tab stop type you selected

3 Adjust the tab stop if you need, by dragging it along the ruler to its new position

① The Tab Alignment button — keep clicking it until the tab stop you want is selected (align left is default)

` L | · | · 1 | · | · 2 · | · 3 | · | · 4 · | · 5 | · | · 6 · | · 7 | · | · 8 · | · 9 | · | · 10 · | · 11 · | · 12 · | · 13 · | · 14 · | 15 · | `

② After selecting a tab stop type, click in the ruler to position your tab stop. The tab stop is displayed by one of four symbols (plus the bar tab symbol)

Old tab position

New tab position

` L | · | · 1 | · | · 2 · | · 3 | · | · 4 · | · 5 | · | · 6 · | · 7 | · | · 8 · | · 9 | · | · 10 · | · 11 · | · 12 · | · 13 · | · 14 · | 15 · | `

¶
└

As you drag, a line shows you the new tab position in the document

③ You can adjust a tab stop's position by dragging it along the ruler to where you want it

Simple tables

To tabulate a simple table you can use tabs. Because tabs are a paragraph format, you need to select the paragraphs which form the table before setting the tabs — in exactly the same ways described when we selected text previously. Once the paragraphs forming the table are selected, the tab changes you make affect all those paragraphs.

Take note:

Never, never, never, never, never (enough to make you see the importance?) press Tab **more than once to align text. It doesn't matter if text doesn't align as you want while you're entering it (see Tip below) — it's still better to change the tabs later to suit your layout requirements. That way you can see the affects of changes you make to the text directly. If you set the tab stops *before* you enter the text, you're just guessing where they need to be, and you'll almost certainly have to change them anyway!**

Basic steps:

1   After you've typed in the paragraphs you want to be tabulated, select them

2   Set your tabs (don't worry if they're not exact — just set them approximately)

3   Adjust the tabs (by dragging them along the ruler to suit) until the text tabulates as you want — by typing text in first using the default tab stops, followed by setting your own tabs then adjusting them, you can see the effects of adjustment on-screen

4   Make any changes to character or other paragraph formats you want

Tip:

Where tab stops have to be set prior to text entry on a typewriter, this is not the case with Word. In fact, it is better simply to enter the text which is to be tabulated before setting tabs at all. The default tabs in a Word document (set at every 1.27 centimetre — half an inch for those old enough to remember) will let you tabulate the text initially (it probably won't align at all as you type it in — but don't worry). Once the text is completely entered you can select it, then put the tab stops where you want. Even once you've set the tab stops you can change them to suit, until you've got the text looking as you want it

(1) Select the paragraphs you want — note the heading of the table isn't selected here

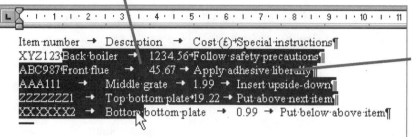

Note how the default tab stops render the table some-what unattractive — it doesn't matter at this stage because step 3 tidies it up

(2)

Set the tabs you want for each column of the table (see pages 54–55)

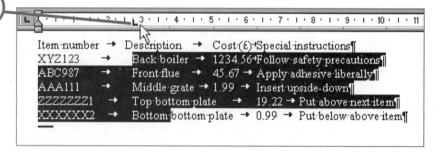

(3) Adjust the tabs to suit the table and the appearance you want

```
Item·number  →  Description  →  Cost·(£)→Special·instructions¶
XYZ123    →   Back·boiler  →  1234.56      →   Follow·safety·precautions¶
ABC987    →   Front·flue   →   45.67       →   Apply·adhesive·liberally¶
AAA111    →   Middle·grate →    1.99       →   Insert·upside-down¶
ZZZZZZZ1  →   Top·bottom·plate →  19.22    →   Put·above·next·item¶
XXXXXX2   →   Bottom·bottom·plate →0.99     →   Put·below·above·item¶
```

Now the heading can be tabulated to suit

(4) Make character and other paragraph formatting changes you want

```
Item·number  →  Description     →     Cost·(£) →  Special·instructions¶
XYZ123    →   Back·boiler   →   1234.56 →  Follow·safety·precautions¶
ABC987    →   Front·flue    →     45.67 →  Apply·adhesive·liberally¶
AAA111    →   Middle·grate  →      1.99 →  Insert·upside-down¶
ZZZZZZZ1  →   Top·bottom·plate →  19.22 →  Put·above·next·item¶
XXXXXX2   →   Bottom·bottom·plate →0.99 →  Put·below·above·item¶
```

More about tabs

While the ruler affords by far the easiest method of setting and adjusting tabs, it is actually quite inexact and some tab options aren't available from it. Total control over tabs (both setting and adjusting) is available from the Tabs dialog box.

1 Display Tabs dialog box by choosing **Format ⤻ Tabs** or by typing Alt + O then T (or by clicking on the Tabs buttons in the Paragraph dialog box — see page 51)

2 Set tab stop positions, alignment types, and leaders (if required)

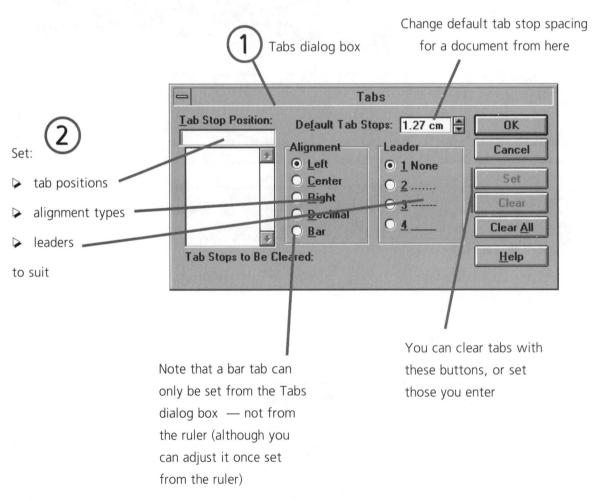

Change default tab stop spacing for a document from here

(1) Tabs dialog box

Set: (2)

▷ tab positions

▷ alignment types

▷ leaders

to suit

Tabs

Tab Stop Position:

Default Tab Stops: 1.27 cm

Alignment
- ● Left
- ○ Center
- ○ Right
- ○ Decimal
- ○ Bar

Leader
- ● 1 None
- ○ 2 ....
- ○ 3 -------
- ○ 4 ___

OK
Cancel
Set
Clear
Clear All
Help

Tab Stops to Be Cleared:

Note that a bar tab can only be set from the Tabs dialog box — not from the ruler (although you can adjust it once set from the ruler)

You can clear tabs with these buttons, or set those you enter

58

There are two options to clear tabs:

1 You can use the clear buttons in the Tabs dialog box (see below left)

2 You can literally drag the tabs off the ruler so they disappear. This is by far the faster method where only a few tabs are to be cleared

Tip:

Tabs – as we've already seen – are paragraph formats. Like all the other paragraph formats they remain in operation after each paragraph, until you change them.

If you want tab settings to remain in operation for a few paragraphs you can set them before you start, then type away. As you press Enter or ⏎ to begin a new paragraph the formats (including tab settings) are carried over

---

Tip:

You can fill the empty space before a tab stop with dotted, dashed, or solid lines called leaders. They can give a professional finish to contents pages, say, where a contents list is separated from its page number list by some considerable space

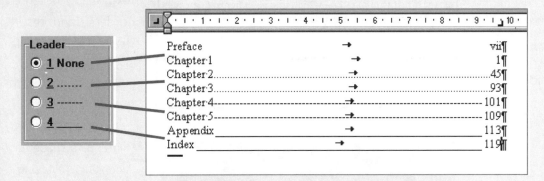

Take note:

You can only set or clear leaders from the Tabs dialog box

Borders and shading

Two other paragraph formats which can be used to create a professional appearance to Word documents are paragraph borders and shading.

Borders are rules around a paragraph (which may, or may not, be thick enough to see — a border of zero thickness is still there, albeit not visible). Shadings are the background shades of colours or greys which go inside borders.

Borders and shadings are set up and adjusted in one of two ways:

● through the Borders toolbar

● with the Paragraph Borders and Shading dialog box.

The easiest way to apply borders and shading is with the Borders toolbar

1 If it's not already displayed, call up the Borders toolbar by clicking the Borders button 🔲 on the Formatting toolbar

How the paragraph is formatted is very important to how the bordered and shaded paragraph will look. Justified or centred text always looks better than left- or right-aligned text, simply because the borders (and resultant shading) are evenly placed around the text

Borders can be:

➢ thinner

➢ thicker

➢ non-existent

> Here is a bordered paragraph — I think it looks really smart. If text is justified — which this is, or centred, it gives a tidy appearance at each side.

> Here is another bordered paragraph — this time though aligned left to see the difference. Not so good, hmm? I agree. However, what do you think of the shading?

> Here is a paragraph with no border but some shading. As the shading is quite dark (60%) the text colour has been reversed to white creating a nice effect.

For a paragraph you intend to shade darkly, consider reversing text to create a pleasant effect

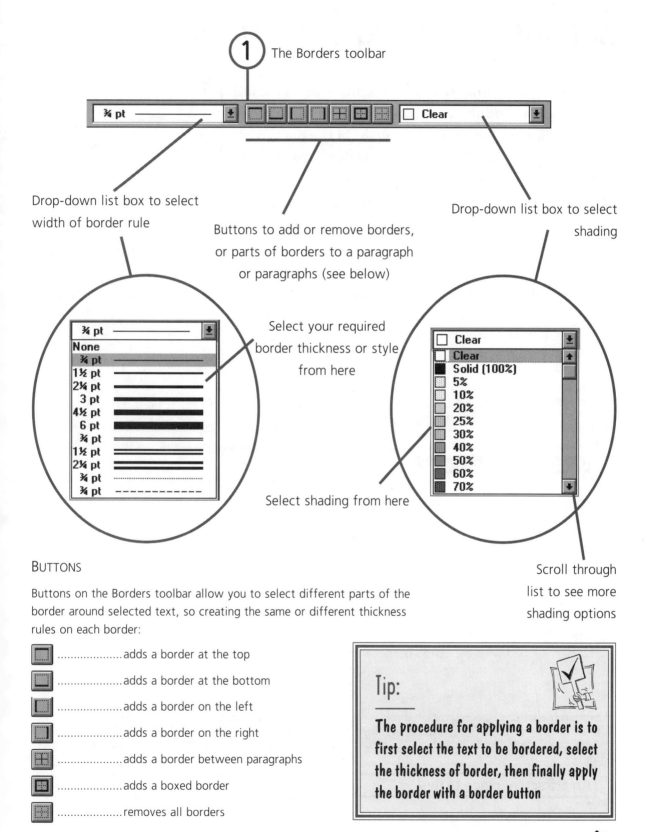

① The Borders toolbar

Drop-down list box to select width of border rule

Buttons to add or remove borders, or parts of borders to a paragraph or paragraphs (see below)

Drop-down list box to select shading

Select your required border thickness or style from here

Select shading from here

BUTTONS

Buttons on the Borders toolbar allow you to select different parts of the border around selected text, so creating the same or different thickness rules on each border:

....................adds a border at the top

....................adds a border at the bottom

....................adds a border on the left

....................adds a border on the right

....................adds a border between paragraphs

....................adds a boxed border

....................removes all borders

Scroll through list to see more shading options

Tip:

The procedure for applying a border is to first select the text to be bordered, select the thickness of border, then finally apply the border with a border button

61

Borders & shading (contd)

When you add a border to text it extends around the full size of the paragraph the text is formatted to. In other words, whatever the width and height of the paragraph will be the width and height of the border — regardless of whether the text itself totally fills the border. This can result in unusual (and unattractive) borders.

① Select the text to have a border — remember (as borders and shades are paragraph formats) you only need to click in the paragraph to select the whole paragraph

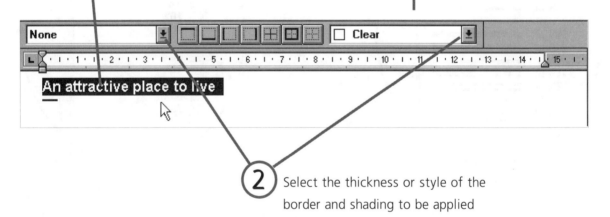

② Select the thickness or style of the border and shading to be applied

Apply the border — this one is a boxed border, applied with the boxed border button ③

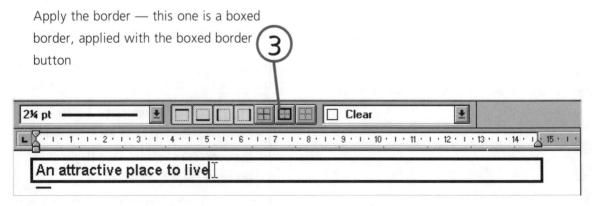

(4) Drag the right indent marker of the ruler in, until the indent is just to the right of the text in the paragraph

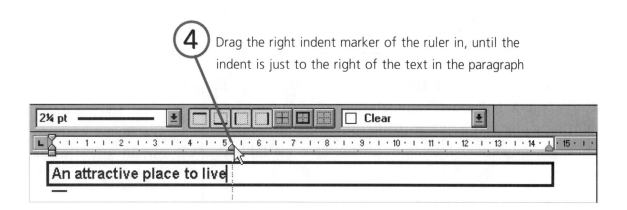

The paragraph is now boxed properly and attractively — note that if you now add to the text in the bordered paragraph the border will still be the correct width as the text simply overflows onto the next line which is of the same width. The border's bottom rule remains below the bottom line of the paragraph however many lines it has

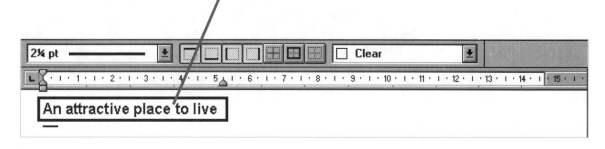

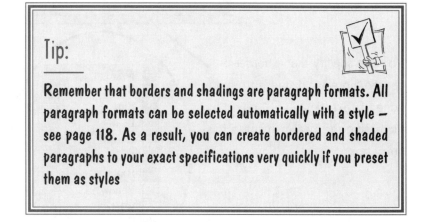

Tip:

Remember that borders and shadings are paragraph formats. All paragraph formats can be selected automatically with a style — see page 118. As a result, you can create bordered and shaded paragraphs to your exact specifications very quickly if you preset them as styles

Borders & shading (contd)

You can create and adjust borders and shadings through the Paragraph Borders and Shading dialog box too. While this isn't as quick as using the Borders toolbar it does provide some options not otherwise available.

1 To call up the Paragraph Borders and Shading dialog box choose
Format→Borders and Shading, or type ⌊Alt⌋+⌊O⌋ then ⌊B⌋

The Paragraph Borders and Shading dialog box

Click this tab to see the shading options (see opposite)

Paragraph Borders and Shading

Some borders are preset — just click the one you want

| Borders | Shading |

Presets

None **Box** **Shadow**

Line
○ **None**

Style:
¾ pt
1½ pt
2¼ pt
3 pt
4½ pt
6 pt
¾ pt
1½ pt
2¼ pt
¾ pt
¾ pt

OK
Cancel
Show Toolbar
Help

Border

Preview shows effects and allows you to select the border (or borders) you want to create — just click on the border you want at the edge of the text in the preview

From Text: 1 pt

Color:
Auto

You can specify that a border is spaced a greater distance from the edge of text (default is 1 point) by increasing the measurement in this entry box

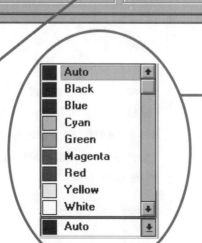

Auto
Black
Blue
Cyan
Green
Magenta
Red
Yellow
White

Auto

Choose the colours of borders from this drop-down list box (see opposite)

Click this tab to get back to borders options

Shading options shown when this tab is clicked

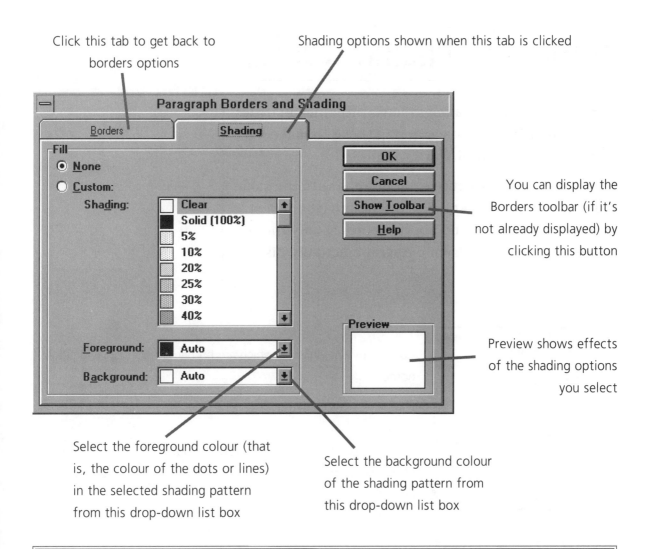

You can display the Borders toolbar (if it's not already displayed) by clicking this button

Preview shows effects of the shading options you select

Select the foreground colour (that is, the colour of the dots or lines) in the selected shading pattern from this drop-down list box

Select the background colour of the shading pattern from this drop-down list box

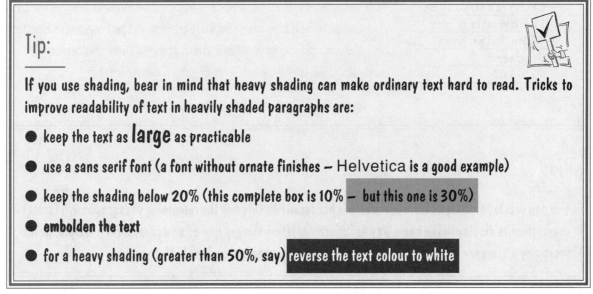

Tip:

If you use shading, bear in mind that heavy shading can make ordinary text hard to read. Tricks to improve readability of text in heavily shaded paragraphs are:

● keep the text as large as practicable

● use a sans serif font (a font without ornate finishes – Helvetica is a good example)

● keep the shading below 20% (this complete box is 10% – but this one is 30%)

● embolden the text

● for a heavy shading (greater than 50%, say) reverse the text colour to white

Borders & shading (contd)

Borders (and their shadings) have three peculiarities in use, and it's worth considering these to make sure you get the best out of Word.

First is the way consecutive paragraphs with the same indents display borders. For example if you select a group of paragraphs and apply a border, only the top paragraph and the bottom paragraph actually display their borders.

```
Christopher Codling
The Hermitage
Whitethorpe Lane
Bolsinger
XX9 1ZZ
```

Consecutive paragraphs which are bordered only display a single border

```
Christopher Codling
The Hermitage
Whitethorpe Lane
Bolsinger
XX9 1ZZ
```

You can specify that only the top and bottom borders are displayed by disabling the left and right borders from the respective buttons on the Borders toolbar

```
Christopher Codling
The Hermitage
Whitethorpe Lane
Bolsinger
XX9 1ZZ
```

You can specify that borders are applied between paragraphs by clicking between the preview paragraphs in the Paragraph Borders and Shading dialog box. Make them thinner than the border outsides (like this example) to create a better effect

Tip:

You can delete paragraphs from text which is bordered like this and the remaining paragraphs will format themselves to display in the same way as before. Deleting the top line of an address, for example, won't make any difference to the border – there'll just be one paragraph less in the group

Second peculiarity is the way borders apply to consecutive paragraphs which have *different* indents. Now, instead of creating what essentially is a single border around all the paragraphs, the paragraphs with different indents each have a separate border — which looks odd enough. What's worse though, as the paragraphs abut each other, the top border of each lower paragraph of a pair effectively disappears. If the lower paragraph of a pair extends beyond the upper paragraph, then the lack of a top border is apparent. The effect is not attractive at all. There are two solutions:

- preferably; give all paragraphs the same indents

- if you can't do that; follow the tip to the right.

Tip:

There *is* a way of creating a single border around such paragraphs – by putting the paragraphs into the cell of a Word table which has just one row and one column (see page 108)

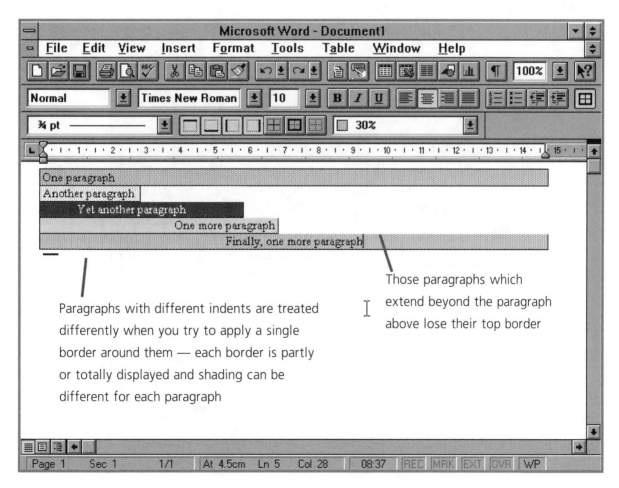

Paragraphs with different indents are treated differently when you try to apply a single border around them — each border is partly or totally displayed and shading can be different for each paragraph

Those paragraphs which extend beyond the paragraph above lose their top border

Borders & shading (contd)

Third peculiarity in the way Word treats borders and shadings is the fact that you can't extend a shade beyond the default distance from the edge of the text unless a border has first been applied, and the distance beyond text has been specified in the From Text entry box of the Borders tab of the Paragraph Borders and Shading dialog box.

The problem arises if you want extended shading without a border rule at all. As soon as you remove the border the shading retreats back to the default distance. There is a method, however, of creating extended shading with no border rule.

1 Select the text to have an extended shading applied, and call up the Paragraph Borders and Shading dialog box (by either choosing **Format**→**Borders and Shading**, or by typing Alt + O then B)

2 Apply the preset box border

① Paragraph Borders and Shading dialog box

⑥ Click the Shading tab, and choose the shade you want

② Click the box border

④ Choose a thin border

③ Specify distance you want the shading to extend from the text

⑤ Choose white in the Colour drop-down list box

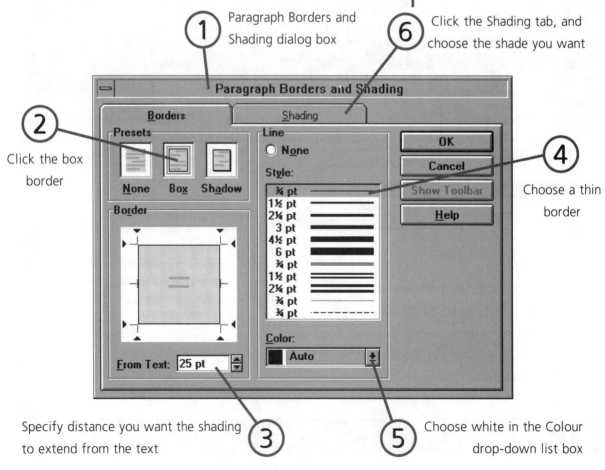

68

3 Specify your desired distance to extend shading in the From Text entry box

4 Choose a thin border (say $^3/_4$ point)

5 Click the colour drop-down list box and select white — to make the thin border white

6 Click the shading tab to view shading options and choose the shade you want the extended border to have (Remember the tips on page 65). Finally, click OK to view the effects

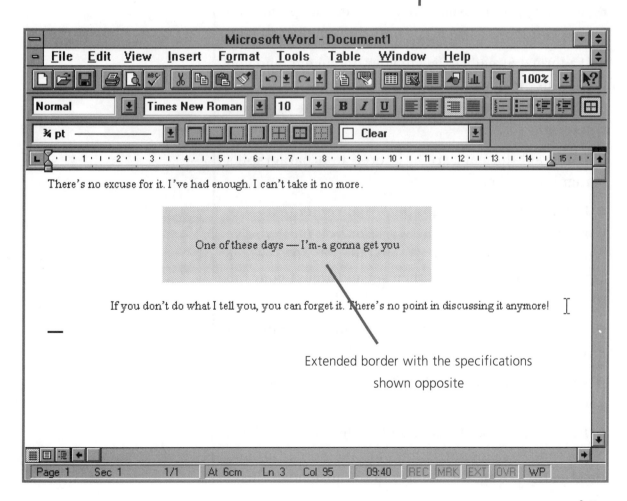

Extended border with the specifications shown opposite

Summary for Section 3

● Both character and paragraph formatting are useful — apply them to selected text by all means — but automatic formatting (using styles and AutoFormatting — covered in Section 6) are even more useful.

● Formatting — whether character formats, paragraph formats, styles or AutoFormats — is the key to producing good-looking effective documents.

● Character and paragraph formats are quickly applied by clicking buttons on the Formatting toolbar — keyboard shortcuts, however, are often even quicker

● If you apply a format to the insertion point, the format continues as you type until you change it again.

● If a format already exists in your document, and you want to use it again, use the Format Painter button on the Standard toolbar to paint the format wherever you want.

● Paragraph formats are all stored in a paragraph's paragraph marker ¶.

● Don't bother setting tabs *before* you enter text — let Word's default tabs do the work for you until you've typed in the text you want to be tabulated. After you've typed it in, select the text then set and adjust your tab to suit.

● Set and adjust tabs from the ruler wherever possible — this is by far the quickest way.

● Use borders and shading to emphasise points in your document.

● Borders (and shading) extends right around the text block — to each indent. If you want the border around *just* the text, bring the indents in to those positions.

4   Sections and pages

About sections

Sometimes when you are working on a document, you need to split it up into smaller parts, without splitting it up into totally different documents. These smaller parts are called *sections.*

You only need to create sections if you want to change the appearance of parts of your document in certain ways. The changes you can make within a document which require that sections have to be created include:

- a different page size

- different margins (page 75)

- a different number of columns (page 84)

- a different header or footer (page 78)

- different line numberings (page 82).

In normal view (and in page layout view if the Show/ Hide ¶ button ¶ on the Standard toolbar is clicked), a section end is displayed as shown below.

A section break, indicated by a dotted line. This does not print

---

The quiet revolution
The personal computer world is in a state of limbo as Intel's domination of the market is about to be challenged

==================================End of Section==================================

Things move pretty quickly where personal computers are concerned. From the dawn of the personal computer era just ten years ago several generations of integrated circuits have come and gone, tens of computer manufacturers have made fortunes and bitten the dust, and just a handful of manufacturers now seems to survive. But that's by no means an end to the story. This year there's the start of what will come to be seen as the biggest shake-up ever known in the industry, with conventions overthrown and market percentages re-negotiated to an extent never seen before. Yet users could be forgiven for not even realising what's going on. Most of the changes have occurred so far in the background, with little noise and a great deal of stealth.

The cause of this quiet revolution is a new microprocessor architecture known as PowerPC. While it's not a name particularly prominent at present to anyone not in the know; it will be. Already PowerPC computers are available, and by the end of this year there'll be a multitude of such personal computers around, capable of running *all* popular applications from any of the major platforms. It's this multi-platform ability which will help PowerPC manufacturers take a bigger slice of the marketing pie than they've been able to have in the past. It's this multi-platform ability which will challenge finally the domination enjoyed for so

Basic steps:

1 Position the insertion point in your document where you want the new section to be, then choose **Insert↱Break**, or type `Alt`+`I` then `B`, to call up the Break dialog box

2 Click the button corresponding to the section break you want:

▷ Next Page — the section break causes the document to force following text to appear at the top of the next page

▷ Even Page — following text is forced to the top of the next even page of the document

▷ Odd page — following text is forced to the top of the next odd page of the document

▷ Continuous — following text occurs straight under the section break, wherever it occurs on a page

3 Click OK

Effectively, the changes listed are parameters you apply much like character and paragraph formats, except they affect the whole section (not just a few characters or paragraphs). Every time you want to change one or more of these parameters in just *part* of your document, you need a new section.

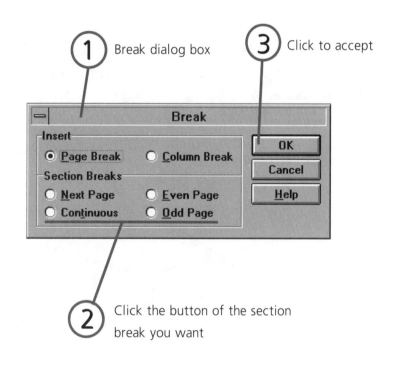

① Break dialog box

③ Click to accept

② Click the button of the section break you want

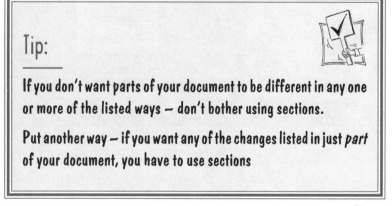

Tip:

If you don't want parts of your document to be different in any one or more of the listed ways – don't bother using sections.

Put another way – if you want any of the changes listed in just *part* of your document, you have to use sections

Setting up a document

Apart from character and paragraph formats, a document has other parameters you can format. Where these are contained within a section (or selected sections) of a document they affect just that section (or sections). Where the document contains no section breaks (that is, the document comprises just one section), or where all sections of a document are selected before formatting, the whole document is affected.

Most of these parameters are adjusted from the Page Setup dialog box, although other methods are sometimes available.

Basic steps:

1. Choose **File→Page Setup**, or type [Alt]+[F] then [U], to call up the Page Setup dialog box
2. Click tabs to see the different controls available to adjust parameters
3. If you make any changes to parameters, click OK to accept changes, or Cancel to ignore them

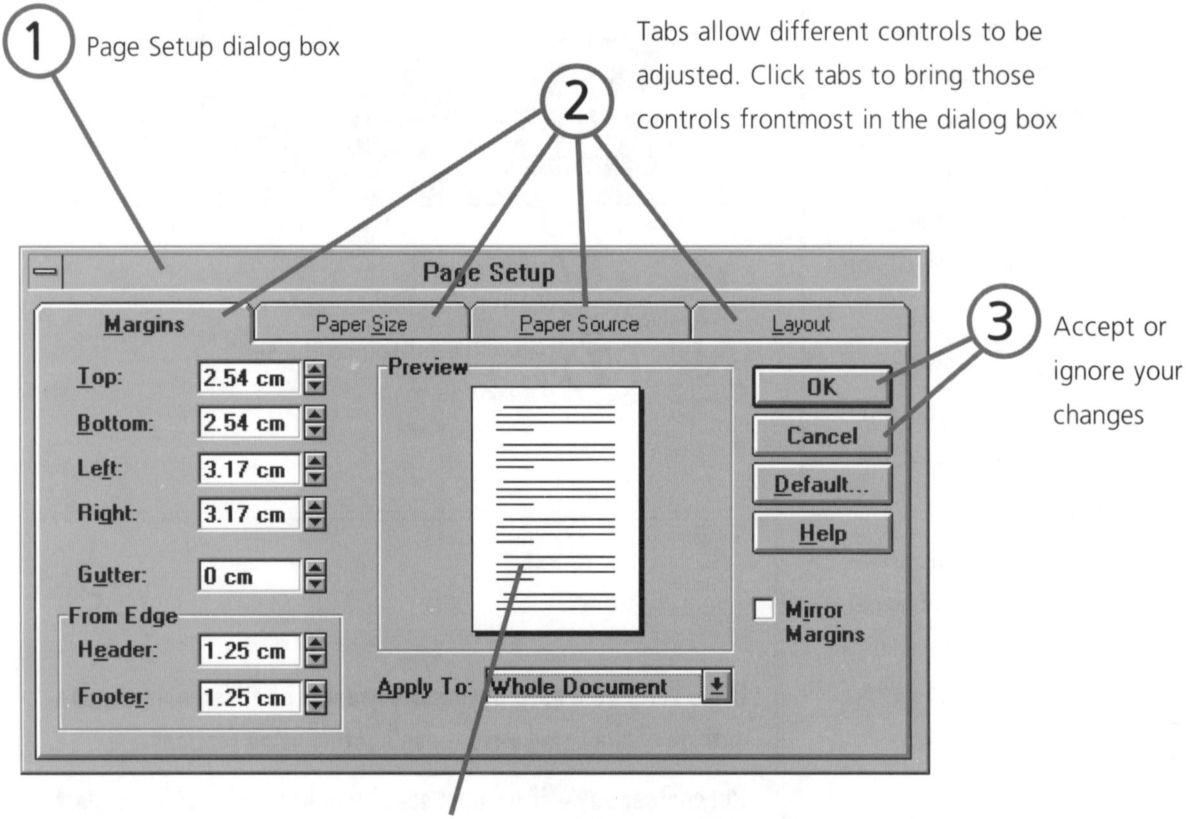
1
Page Setup dialog box
2
Tabs allow different controls to be adjusted. Click tabs to bring those controls frontmost in the dialog box
3
Accept or ignore your changes
Page Setup
Margins
Paper Size
Paper Source
Layout
Top: 2.54 cm
Bottom: 2.54 cm
Left: 3.17 cm
Right: 3.17 cm
Gutter: 0 cm
From Edge
Header: 1.25 cm
Footer: 1.25 cm
Preview
Apply To: Whole Document
OK
Cancel
Default...
Help
Mirror Margins

Preview of your document's overall appearance with parameters as you set them in the dialog box

Margins

Margins are imaginary guides on a document page, outside of which text isn't normally situated. By default, Word creates margins for any new document — usually of 2.54 cm from top and bottom of the page (1 inch, if you're old enough to remember), and 3.17 cm from left and right page edge (1.25 inches).

You can change margins, either for a whole document or for a section, from the Page Setup dialog box.

Basic steps:

1 Choose **File→Page Setup**, or type [Alt]+[F] then [U], to call up the Page Setup dialog box

2 Click the Margins tab if it's not already frontmost (see opposite)

3 Adjust margin dimensions to suit

> ## Tip:
>
> In many of these tabs (and in many other dialog boxes, for that matter) adjustments can be made to some controls by increasing or decreasing in preset steps by clicking on the up or down arrows to the right of the entry boxes. Alternatively, you can click on the entry box you want to change then enter the exact value you want

> ## Tip:
>
> You can specify that the margin changes be applied to just the section you are in, from the current point on (Word places a section break at the insertion point and changes apply to the section following it), or the whole document, from the drop-down list box on the Margins tab of the Page Setup dialog box
>
>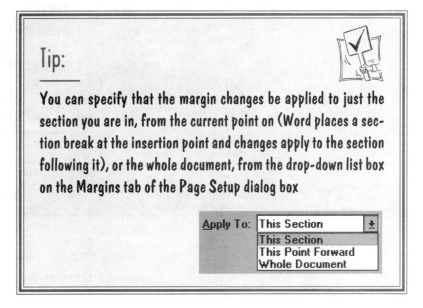

Margins (contd)

Some of the controls of the Margins tab of the Page Setup dialog box allow you to control how pages are printed for double-sided purposes (that is, for the likes of books and reports).

1 If the document is to be double-sided, check the Mirror Margins check box

2 Change the Inside and Outside margins measurements to suit your requirements

3 If the you plan to bind your document with a ring or similar method, enter a value in the Gutter entry box — this gives extra space inside the inside margins to allow for the binding

If Mirror Margins check box is checked, these entry boxes change to show Inside and Outside margin measurements

Preview always shows the effects of entries and controls

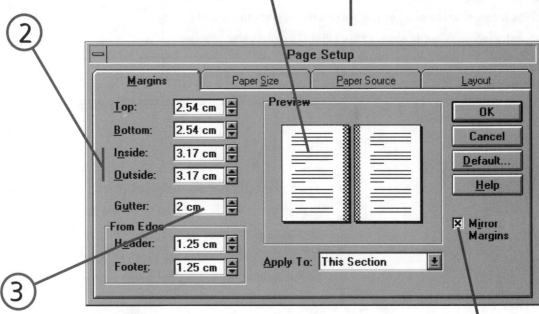

Entering a value here creates an extra space to allow for a binding

Check here for margins which are equal on the insides, and equal on the outsides of each left and right hand page

Basic steps:

1 Choose **View** → **Page Layout**, or type `Alt` + `V` then `P`, or (best) click the Page Layout button 📄 to view your document in page layout view

2 Drag your margins to suit

As an alternative to using the Page Setup dialog box, you can adjust margins by dragging margin boundaries in page layout view (or print preview — see page 142). This is probably faster, though you have little accuracy, you can't specify how much of the document you want to apply changes to (current section, current point forward, or the whole document — dragging from the ruler applies changes to just the current section, or whole document if no section break exists), and mirror margin and gutter margin controls aren't available.

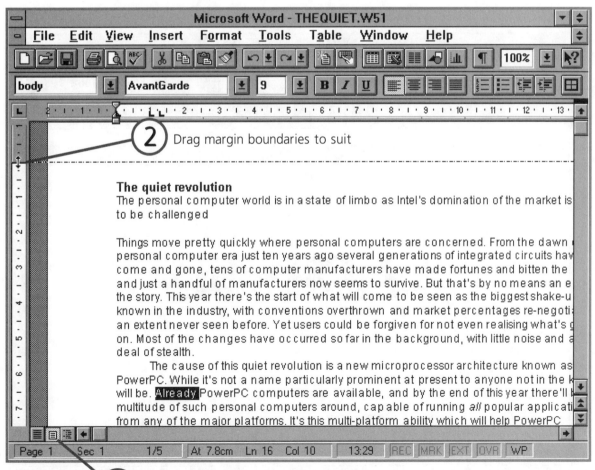

② Drag margin boundaries to suit

① Click here if document is not already in page layout view

Headers and footers

A header is a heading (often called a running head) which appears at the top of each page in a document or section of a document. A footer is at the bottom of each page. You can put text or graphical items in either and you can format them in the usual ways.

Basic steps:

1 To create either a header or a footer choose **View ↳Header and Footer**, or type Alt + V then H. The document changes to page layout view and displays the header entry box and the Header and Footer toolbar

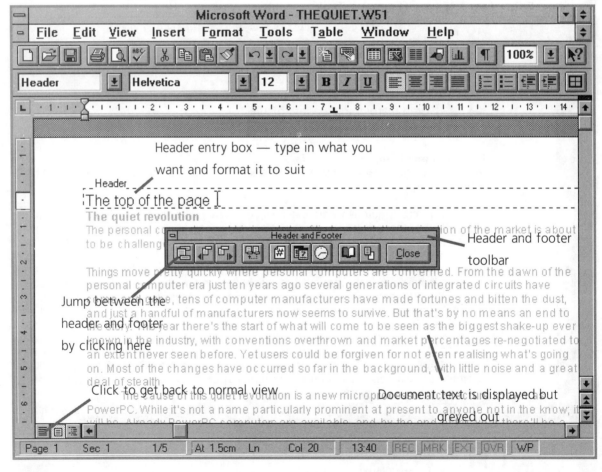

Header entry box — type in what you want and format it to suit

Header
The top of the page

Header and footer toolbar

Jump between the header and footer by clicking here

Click to get back to normal view

Document text is displayed but greyed out

78

Tip:

Your document's text is displayed grey when in Headers and Footers view. Double-click anywhere in the text, however, and the text becomes active (sending the headers and footers to a greyed background outline). You can switch between the two by double-clicking each in this way

Tip:

Headers and footers apply to individual sections – in other words, you can have different headers and footers for each section if you want

Double-click on a greyed header to make it active

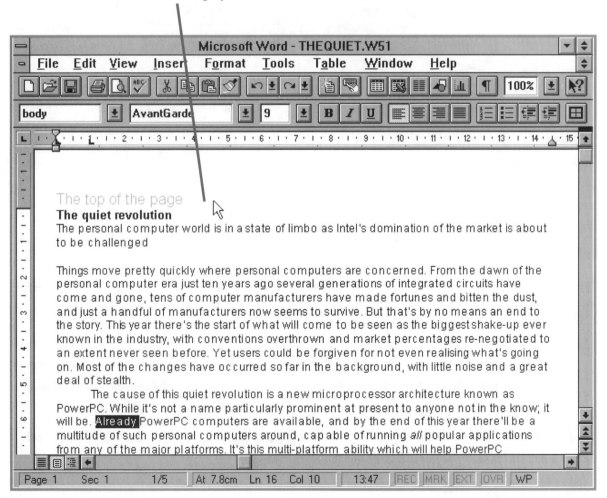

Headers & footers (contd)

The Headers and Footers toolbar has a number of buttons. Use these to access various features and entries you can make into a header or footer.

Page Setup button — calls up the Page Setup dialog box

Switch Between Header and Footer button — click to move from a header to a footer or back (alternatively, you can scroll down or up the page in the document window

Show/Hide Document Text button — jumps between document text and header or footer text

Close — click when you no longer need the Headers and Footers toolbar

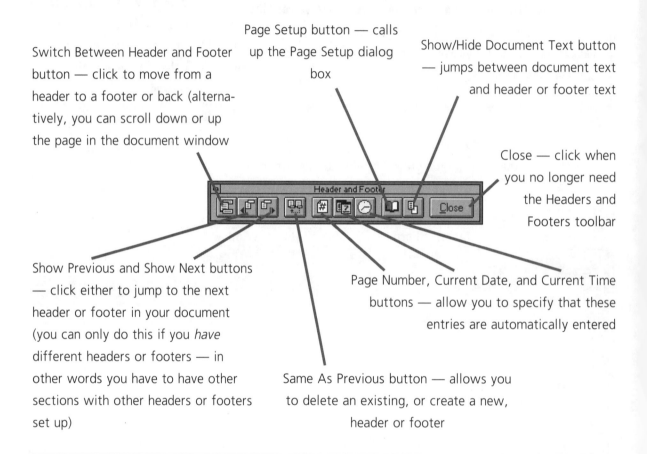

Show Previous and Show Next buttons — click either to jump to the next header or footer in your document (you can only do this if you *have* different headers or footers — in other words you have to have other sections with other headers or footers set up)

Page Number, Current Date, and Current Time buttons — allow you to specify that these entries are automatically entered

Same As Previous button — allows you to delete an existing, or create a new, header or footer

Tip:

Remember you can format a header or a footer in exactly the same way you format ordinary document text. You can embolden, italicise, underline and so on. You can make it centrally aligned or right aligned if you want. You are not restricted to just one line of text. You can also use a graphical item.

Also remember that each section you create can have its own header and footer — use this feature to set up a header for each chapter of a large document, for example

Basic steps:

1 Choose **View→Page Layout**, or type `Alt`+`V` then `P`, or (best) click the Page Layout button `▤` to view your document in page layout view

2 Drag margin and header (or footer) boundaries to suit

You can adjust the distance from a page edge taken up by a header at the top of your document page (or the footer at the bottom) from the Page Setup dialog box (the From Edge entries). You can also change margins from here (allowing you to adjust the distance between the header or footer and the document text.

An easier way, however, is to switch to page layout view and drag the various boundaries to suit what you want.

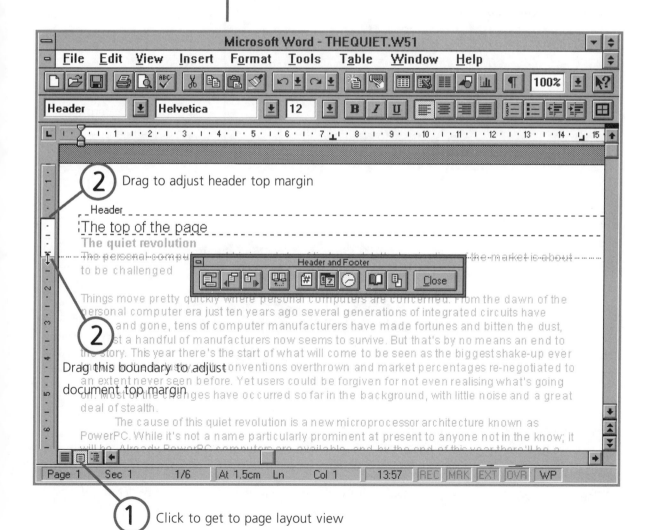

81

Line numbers

Word can display and print line numbers alongside text. This can be useful in technical documentation, and even required in legal literature.

Line numbers are:

● printed in the left margin

● numbered excluding lines in tables, headers, footers and some other parts of a document

● only visible on-screen in page layout view (or print preview — see page 142).

● only visible on-screen in page layout view (or print preview — see page 142).

Basic steps:

1 Choose **File→Page Setup**, or type ⌈Alt⌉+⌈F⌉ then ⌊U⌋ to call up the Page Setup dialog box. Click the Layout tab if it's not already frontmost. Next click the Line Numbers button to call up the Line Numbers dialog box

2 Check the Add Line Numbering check box to create line numbers

3 Adjust controls to suit and click OK to accept and view line numbers

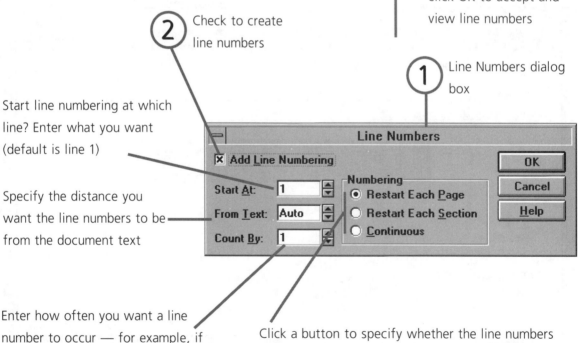

② Check to create line numbers

① Line Numbers dialog box

Start line numbering at which line? Enter what you want (default is line 1)

Specify the distance you want the line numbers to be from the document text

Enter how often you want a line number to occur — for example, if you only want a line number every 10 lines — 10, 20, 30 and so on — enter 10

Click a button to specify whether the line numbers restart at the top of each page; restart at the beginning of each section in the document; or are continuous throughout

82

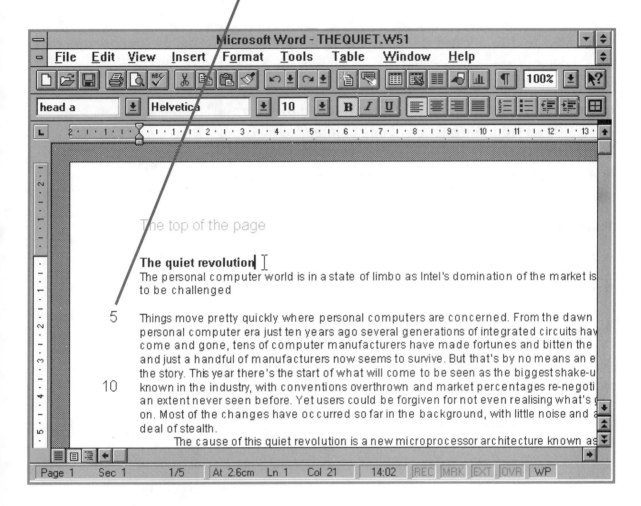

③ Line numbers are visible in page layout (or print preview) views only

To change the format of line numbers you have to redefine the Line Number style — see section 6 for information about styles

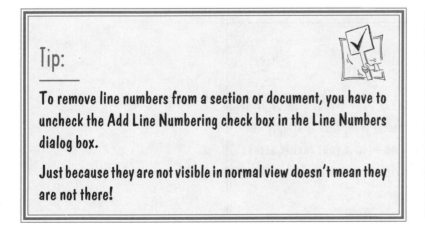

Tip:

To remove line numbers from a section or document, you have to uncheck the Add Line Numbering check box in the Line Numbers dialog box.

Just because they are not visible in normal view doesn't mean they are not there!

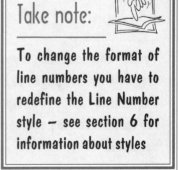

Take note:

To change the format of line numbers you have to redefine the Line Number style — see section 6 for information about styles

Columns

Generally, text in a Word document is in a single col-umn — that is, a single vertical division down the page. You can, however, create two or more columns of text quite simply, where columns are unattached or where a story flows from the bottom of one column to the top of the next. Columns can be used to create newspaper-style or newsletter-style documents, or indeed books such as this one.

You can create columns in your document from either:

● a button on the Standard toolbar; or

● the Columns dialog box.

1 Select the text you want to be formatted into columns, then click the Columns button 📊 on the Standard toolbar

2 Drag across the drop-down window to select the number of columns you want

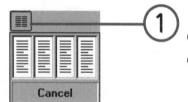

① Click the Columns button to display this drop-down window

Drag across to select the number of columns you want — let go the mouse button to accept

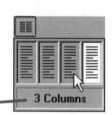

②

Take note:

You can only see columns you create in page layout view or print preview view (see page 142)! In normal view, text is simply dis-played at the width of a *single* column — so if your text is across two columns on the page, normally viewed text willonly be half a page wide

Basic steps:

FROM THE COLUMNS DIALOG BOX

1 Select the text you want
to be formatted into
columns, then choose
Format↳Columns to
call up the Columns dialog
box

2 Choose the number of
coumns you want

3 Change column widths and
other controls to suit your
requirements

Tip:

If you select text then format it into columns, Word automatically
inserts section breaks before and after the text. This way you can
have different numbers of columns in different parts of the document – columns are section parameters, remember

If you simply position the insertion point in your document before
formatting into columns (that is, you *don't* select any text), the
whole section (the whole *document* if no section breaks are present
in the document) is formatted

① Columns dialog box

Click to select the
number of columns
from these buttons, or
enter the number in the
lower box ②

③

Adjust column widths to suit

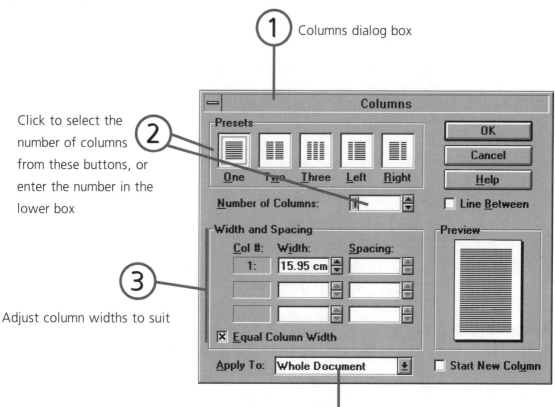

Specify which part of document to apply columns to
(whole document, current section, or from this point on)

85

Columns (contd)

If you want to format your section or document into even-width columns, the quickest method is with the Columns button on the Standard toolbar.

On the other hand, if you want *uneven* columns you have to use the Columns dialog box. The Columns dialog box also gives some other controls unavailable with the Columns button:

● the spacing between columns

● whether a line between columns is displayed

● whether the columns apply to the whole document, the current section, or from the current point on.

Tip:

If you want multi-column text underneath single column text first enter text without any column formatting. Next, select the text to be multi-column formatted and format it. Word automatically creates section breaks before and after the multi-column formatted section

Click here to give two columns of unequal width — measurements in the width entry boxes are automatically adjusted to suit

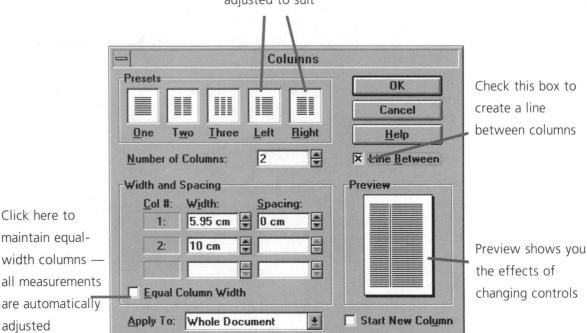

Check this box to create a line between columns

Click here to maintain equal-width columns — all measurements are automatically adjusted

Preview shows you the effects of changing controls

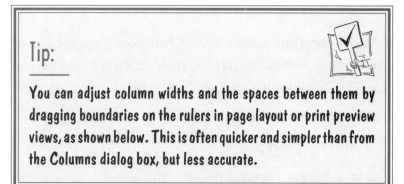

Tip:

You can adjust column widths and the spaces between them by dragging boundaries on the rulers in page layout or print preview views, as shown below. This is often quicker and simpler than from the Columns dialog box, but less accurate.

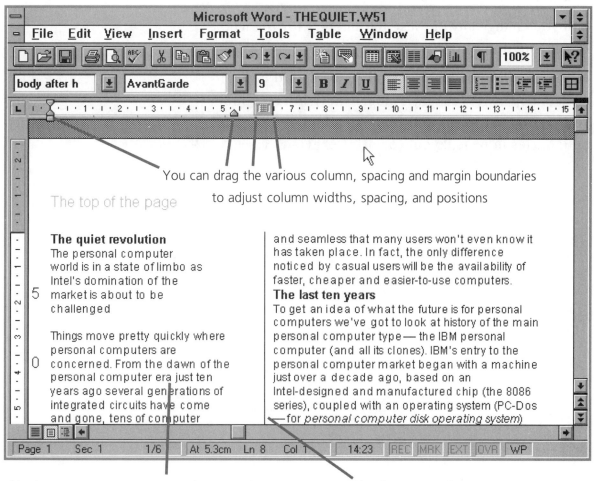

You can drag the various column, spacing and margin boundaries to adjust column widths, spacing, and positions

The top of the page

The quiet revolution
The personal computer world is in a state of limbo as Intel's domination of the market is about to be challenged

Things move pretty quickly where personal computers are concerned. From the dawn of the personal computer era just ten years ago several generations of integrated circuits have come and gone, tens of computer

and seamless that many users won't even know it has taken place. In fact, the only difference noticed by casual users will be the availability of faster, cheaper and easier-to-use computers.

The last ten years
To get an idea of what the future is for personal computers we've got to look at history of the main personal computer type— the IBM personal computer (and all its clones). IBM's entry to the personal computer market began with a machine just over a decade ago, based on an Intel-designed and manufactured chip (the 8086 series), coupled with an operating system (PC-Dos —for *personal computer disk operating system*)

This document was setup using the controls as entered in the Columns dialog box shown opposite

Line between columns

Summary for Section 4

● Use a section where you need to change certain parameters for only *part* of your document. The parameters for which a section has to be created include:

- ❑ a different page size

- ❑ different margins

- ❑ a different number of columns

- ❑ a different header or footer

- ❑ different line numberings.

● If you change any of these parameters for *the whole document,* don't use a section.

● Create margins, headers and footers, and columns from dialog boxes (as this is most exact), but remember you can adjust them and their spacings by dragging boundaries in page layout (or print preview) view.

5 Control over text

Finding text

Although it probably sounds odd, one of the main jobs a word processor is asked to do in everyday life is to find text. You'd think a word processor had enough coping with all it's asked to do with text without having to actually find the stuff for you too, wouldn't you?

Problem is, in long documents it's not always easy for us to locate specific instances of small pieces of text. Let's say you have worked for weeks and weeks on your latest novel, and you decide that little bit around half way through about your heroine's home town Dogsbone-in-Coverdale needs expanding somewhat. What do you do? You could scroll through the book, screen-by-screen, trying to find where the town is mentioned, but that could take hours — you wrote it weeks ago remember — and you haven't a baldy exactly where it is.

Let Word do the job for you.

Bear in mind, though, that text in Word doesn't just comprise the individual letters you type in at the keyboard. As we've seen in other sections, text can be formatted with bold, italic and other character formats. It can have paragraph formats applied to it. It can be sectioned and have columns, line numbers, different margins and so on.

The Find command in Word can find any format which you care to apply to text, so is extremely powerful. You can even ask Word to check for words which *sound* similar.

Basic steps:

1 Choose **Edit→Find**, or type `Alt` + `E` then `F`, or type `Ctrl` + `F`. This calls up the Find dialog box

2 In the Find What entry box, type in the text you want to locate

3 Specify the controls you want to control the search

4 Click the Find Next button to start the search

Tip:

When Word finds your text it leaves the Find dialog box open for further searches. Just click (again) the Find Next button to get Word to look again for your selected text. If the dialog box is in your way you can move it around by dragging its title bar, and close it when you've finished

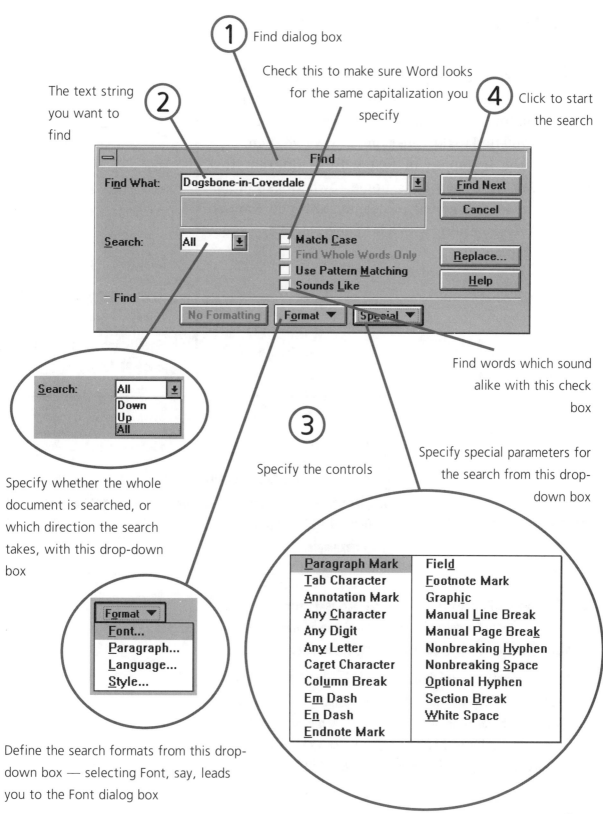

① Find dialog box

Check this to make sure Word looks for the same capitalization you specify

The text string you want to find

②

④ Click to start the search

Find

Fi**nd** What: Dogsbone-in-Coverdale

Find Next

Cancel

Search: All

☐ Match **C**ase
☐ Find Whole Words Only
☐ Use Pattern **M**atching
☐ **S**ounds Like

Replace...

Help

— Find —

No Formatting | **F**ormat ▼ | Spe**c**ial ▼

Search: All
Down
Up
All

Find words which sound alike with this check box

③ Specify the controls

Specify special parameters for the search from this drop-down box

Specify whether the whole document is searched, or which direction the search takes, with this drop-down box

Format ▼
Font...
Paragraph...
Language...
Style...

Paragraph Mark | Fiel**d**
Tab Character | **F**ootnote Mark
Annotation Mark | Grap**h**ic
Any **C**haracter | Manual **L**ine Break
Any Digit | Manual Page Brea**k**
Any **L**etter | Nonbreaking **H**yphen
Ca**r**et Character | Nonbreaking **S**pace
Col**u**mn Break | **O**ptional Hyphen
E**m** Dash | Section **B**reak
E**n** Dash | **W**hite Space
Endnote Mark

Define the search formats from this drop-down box — selecting Font, say, leads you to the Font dialog box

Replacing

In the Find dialog box you may have noticed a button marked Replace. Clicking this leads you to the Replace dialog box (or you can call up the dialog box directly). This lets you find text in the same way we've seen, then replaces the instances of text with a different text string. Say, your heroine's home town Dogsbone-in-Coverdale doesn't sound too canny, and you want to change it to something with a bit more zing. Easy — get Word to replace it.

Basic steps:

1. Choose **Edit→Replace**, or type Alt+E then E, or type Ctrl+H, or (as we've seen) click the Replace button in the Find dialog box. This calls up the Replace dialog box
2. Enter the text string to look for
3. Type in the text string to replace it
4. Specify the controls (see page 91 for details)

Take note:

As you specify a format in either the Find dialog box or the Replace dialog box, the format is shown in the Format box directly below the Find What and Replace With entry boxes (see opposite for example)

Tip:

While Word will happily find and replace text strings for you (formatted or unformatted) it is equally at home finding and replacing just formats (without any text string associated with them).

So, for example, you can find instances of text which are underlined (<u>a typical typists' method of emphasising text</u>) and replace them all with italicised text (*the usual typographers' emphasis method*) by specifying the formats to suit. Remember not to enter any text in either of the Find What or Replace With entry boxes

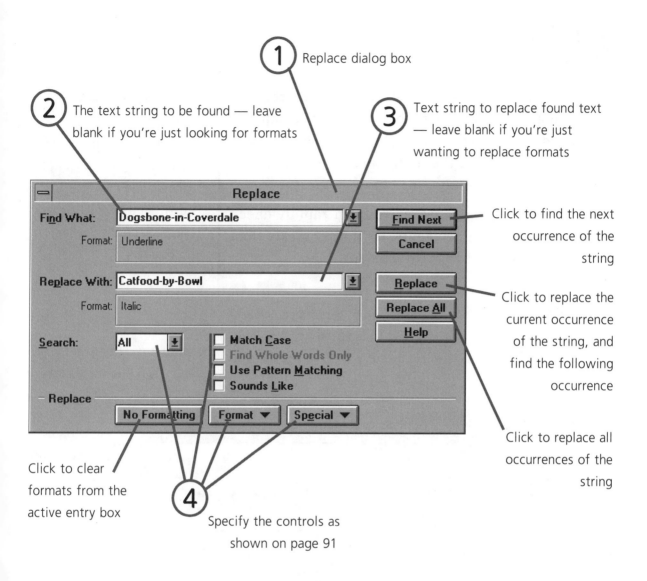

① Replace dialog box

② The text string to be found — leave blank if you're just looking for formats

③ Text string to replace found text — leave blank if you're just wanting to replace formats

Replace

Fi**n**d What: `Dogsbone-in-Coverdale`

Format: Underline

Re**p**lace With: `Catfood-by-Bowl`

Format: Italic

Search: `All`

☐ Match **C**ase
☐ Find Whole Words Only
☐ Use Pattern **M**atching
☐ Sounds **L**ike

Replace

No Formatting   **Format ▼**   **Special ▼**

Find Next
Cancel
Replace
Replace All
Help

Click to find the next occurrence of the string

Click to replace the current occurrence of the string, and find the following occurrence

Click to replace all occurrences of the string

Click to clear formats from the active entry box

④ Specify the controls as shown on page 91

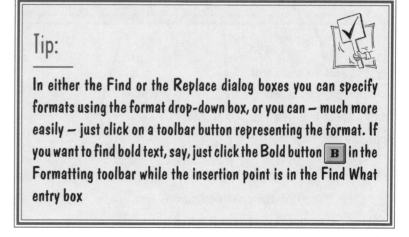

Tip:

In either the Find or the Replace dialog boxes you can specify formats using the format drop-down box, or you can — much more easily — just click on a toolbar button representing the format. If you want to find bold text, say, just click the Bold button **B** in the Formatting toolbar while the insertion point is in the Find What entry box

Spelling

One of Word's most useful tools is a spelling checker which looks through your document and compares each word with the words in an electronic dictionary. If Word finds a word in the dictionary, it assumes that word is spelled correctly.

Using Word's spelling checker you can rapidly check even the longest of documents, far more quickly than you could read through the document.

Basic steps:

1 Choose **Tools⤷Spelling**, or type ⌨Alt+⌨T then ⌨S, or type ⌨F7, or (best) click the Spelling button 🔤 on the Standard toolbar to perform the spelling check and call up the Spelling dialog box

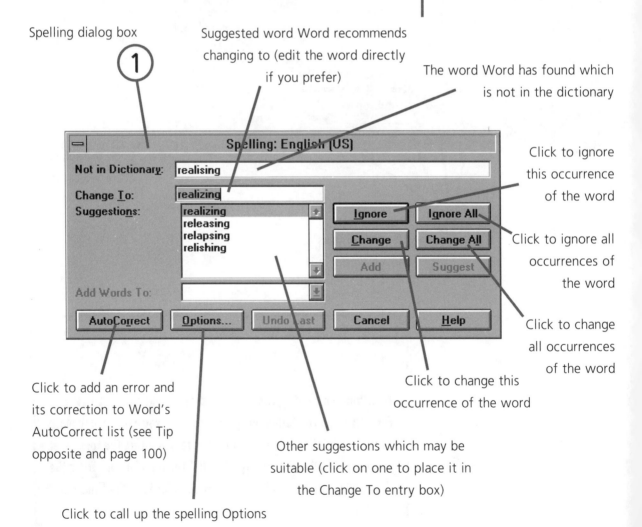

Spelling dialog box

Suggested word Word recommends changing to (edit the word directly if you prefer)

The word Word has found which is not in the dictionary

Click to ignore this occurrence of the word

Click to ignore all occurrences of the word

Click to change all occurrences of the word

Click to change this occurrence of the word

Other suggestions which may be suitable (click on one to place it in the Change To entry box)

Click to add an error and its correction to Word's AutoCorrect list (see Tip opposite and page 100)

Click to call up the spelling Options dialog box (see opposite)

94

In the Options dialog box (with Spelling tab frontmost) you can control Word's spelling options

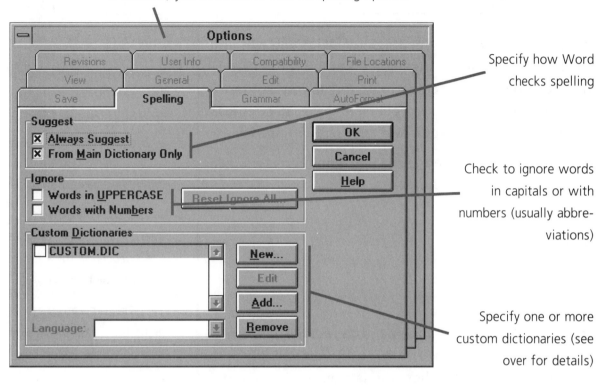

Specify how Word checks spelling

Check to ignore words in capitals or with numbers (usually abbreviations)

Specify one or more custom dictionaries (see over for details)

Options

Revisions	User Info	Compatibility	File Locations
View	General	Edit	Print
Save	**Spelling**	Grammar	AutoFormat

Suggest
- [X] A_lways Suggest
- [X] From _Main Dictionary Only

Ignore
- [ ] Words in _UPPERCASE
- [ ] Words with Num_bers

Reset Ignore All...

Custom _Dictionaries
- [ ] CUSTOM.DIC

New...
Edit
Add...
Remove

Language:

OK
Cancel
Help

Take note:

While Word's spelling checker is an extremely useful tool, you must remember that it only compares words in your document with the words in an electronic list called a dictionary. If the words in your document are mis-spelled in-context but in fact make properly spelled words out-of-context, Word *still* assumes they are spelled correctly. Thus, Word thinks *with complements* (instead of *with compliments*) is OK. Remember the anonymous ode:

I have a spelling checker – it came with my pea see
It plainly marques four my revue mistakes eye cannot sea
I've run this poem threw it, I'm shore your pleased too no
Its let a perfect inn it's weigh – my checquer told me sew

Tip:

Spelling can be corrected automatically in Word, if you consistently seem to make the same spelling errors.

AutoCorrect is a feature whereby you tell Word the mistake you often make, and it corrects it for you whenever you make it. See page 100 for details

Spelling (contd)

When you use Word's Spelling command you can add words which aren't in the main dictionary, to customize Word to your specifications. But if you use more than just a handful of specialised terms it becomes preferable to create your own custom dictionaries.

Examples of specialised terms you would create a custom dictionary for include:

● acronyms

● abbreviations

● technical jargon

● proper names.

If you work in more than one or two specialised areas — let's say you type for two or three different people, one who is a scientist, another who is a marketing person, and so on, it's possible that you need to use more than one custom dictionary.

CREATING A DICTIONARY

1 From the Options dialog box with the Spelling tab frontmost (see previous page), click New. This calls up the Create Custom Dictionary dialog box

2 Enter a dictionary name (make it something obvious like *science.dic* for a scientific dictionary)

3 Click OK to create the dictionary and return you to the Options dialog box.

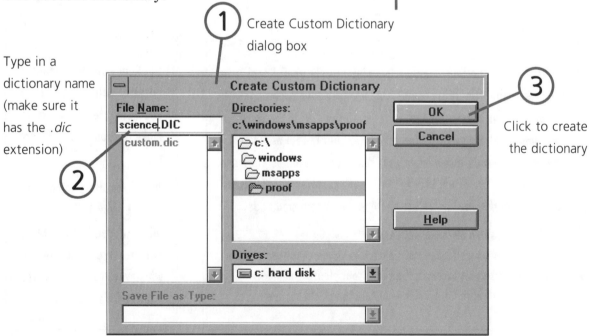

① Create Custom Dictionary dialog box

Type in a dictionary name (make sure it has the .*dic* extension) ②

③ Click to create the dictionary

Create Custom Dictionary

File Name: science.DIC
custom.dic

Directories: c:\windows\msapps\proof
📁 c:\
📁 windows
📁 msapps
📁 proof

OK
Cancel
Help

Drives: 💾 c: hard disk

Save File as Type:

EDITING A DICTIONARY

1 Choose **Tools→Options**, or type [Alt]+[T] then [O], to call up the Options dialog box. Click the Spelling tab to bring it frontmost, select the dictionary and click Edit. Click Yes in the resultant dialog box to open the dictionary. Click OK in the Options dialog box

2 Now review and edit the dictionary as a Word document

3 Save the file as a normal Word document when you have edited it

Take note:

If you have more than one custom dictionary, make sure the one you want to add new words to is open (that is, it should be checked in the Options dialog box)

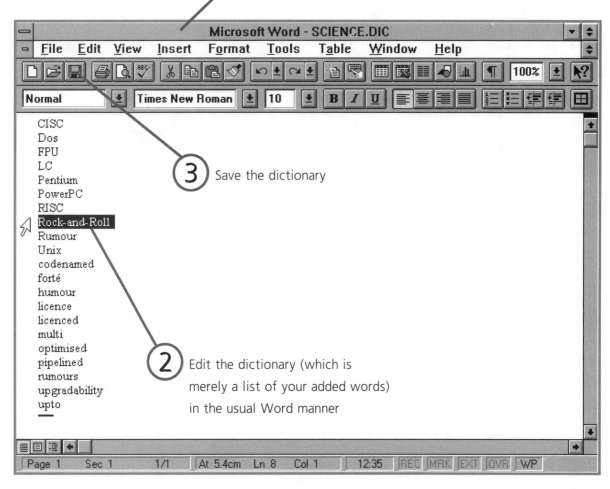

① A dictionary opened for editing

③ Save the dictionary

② Edit the dictionary (which is merely a list of your added words) in the usual Word manner

Thesaurus

Word has an on-line thesaurus to aid editing. This can be extremely useful when writing too, as it gives synonyms quickly, and for some words — antonyms and related words, too.

Basic steps:

1 Select the word you want to find a synonym, antonym or related word for

2 To call up the Thesaurus dialog box, choose **Tools↳Thesaurus**, or type Alt + T then T, or type Shift + F7

Word you selected from your document is entered here

2 Thesaurus dialog box

Click to replace the word originally selected

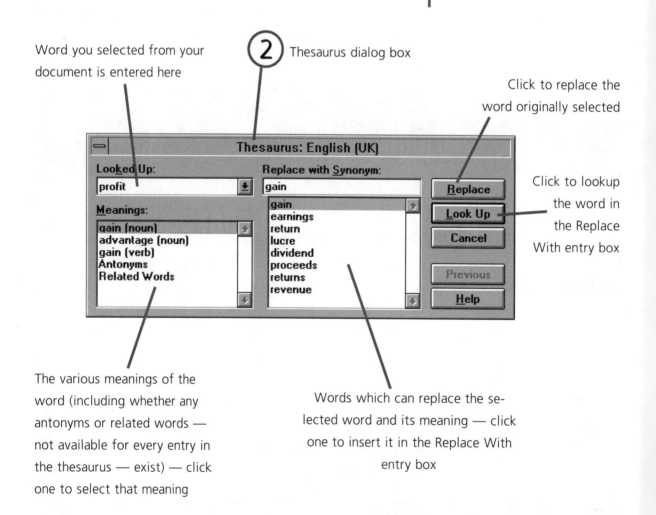

Thesaurus: English (UK)

Looked Up:
profit

Replace with Synonym:
gain

Meanings:
gain (noun)
advantage (noun)
gain (verb)
Antonyms
Related Words

gain
earnings
return
lucre
dividend
proceeds
returns
revenue

Replace
Look Up
Cancel
Previous
Help

Click to lookup the word in the Replace With entry box

The various meanings of the word (including whether any antonyms or related words — not available for every entry in the thesaurus — exist) — click one to select that meaning

Words which can replace the selected word and its meaning — click one to insert it in the Replace With entry box

Grammar

Word's grammar checker may aid your use of English. It operates in much the same way as checking spelling (see page 94) and can help to eliminate those instances of words mis-spelt in-context, leading to out-of-context proper spelling which spelling checkers cannot cope with. For example, spelling checkers cannot differentiate between *compliments* and *complements*, whereas a grammar checker can (see below).

1 To call up the Grammar dialog box choose **Tools↪Grammar**, or type Alt + T then G

1 Grammar dialog box — a sentence at a time is checked

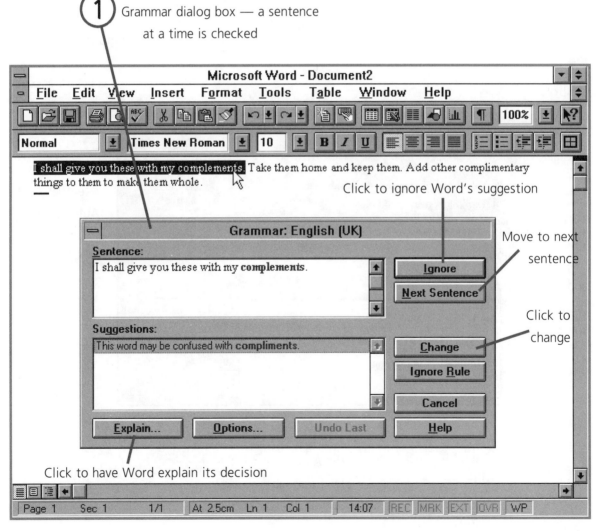

Click to ignore Word's suggestion

Move to next sentence

Click to change

Click to have Word explain its decision

AutoCorrect

If you make the same spelling mistake regularly — say you always type *anf* instead of *and* (the author's problem; well, one of his problems, anyway) — Word's AutoCorrect feature is a boon.

To use AutoCorrect you simply have to specify which mistakes you make, and the correct spelling. Then whenever you make the mistake it is replaced automatically with the correct word.

Basic steps:

1 Call up the AutoCorrect dialog box by choosing **Tools↳AutoCorrect**, or type ⌐Alt⌐+⌐T⌐ then ⌐A⌐

2 Type in the spelling mistake you often make into the Replace entry box, and the proper spelling in the With entry box

3 Click Add to add the word to the AutoCorrect list

AutoCorrect dialog box

Check to turn AutoCorrect on — uncheck to turn it off

Other controls

Click to accept

Click to add your entries to the AutoCorrect list

Mistake you often make, and proper spelling

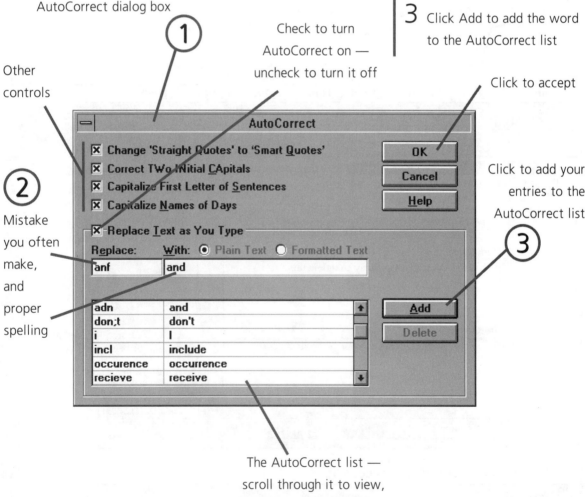

AutoCorrect

☒ Change 'Straight Quotes' to 'Smart Quotes'
☒ Correct TWo INitial CApitals
☒ Capitalize First Letter of Sentences
☒ Capitalize Names of Days

☒ Replace Text as You Type

Replace: With: ● Plain Text ○ Formatted Text

| anf | and |

adn	and
don;t	don't
i	I
incl	include
occurence	occurrence
recieve	receive

OK
Cancel
Help

Add
Delete

The AutoCorrect list — scroll through it to view, edit and delete entries

Tip:

Remember that you can create an AutoCorrect entry direct from the Spelling dialog box (page 94).

If you find that Word is finding the same spelling error repeatedly, click the AutoCorrect button on the Spelling dialog box to enter it into the AutoCorrect list automatically

Tip:

AuotCorrect can be used to insert chunks of text into a document when you type a simple keyword. For example, a phrase like *Yours sincerely,* at the end of a letter can have a keyword such as *ys.* As you type *ys* and hit the or ↵ key, Word automatically replaces it with the longer phrase.

Phrases upto 255 characters (including spaces and punctuation) are possible, so a considerable amount of *boilerplate text* (as it's known in the computer business) can be accessed using AuotCorrect. For longer boilerplate text, and items you access less frequently, use Word's AutoText feature instead of AutoCorrect (see over)

Take note:

Word detects when you have finished a word — hence knows when to replace it, if it has an AutoCorrect entry — when an end-of-word specifier (usually a space) occurs.

So if the spelling error is followed by another letter, Word doesn't recognise the mistake and cannot correct it with AutoCorrect

Tip:

Not only text can be replaced by AutoCorrect entries. Graphics can be included; as can all formatting such as emboldening, sections, borders and shades and so on.

Put your company letterhead into an AutoCorrect entry, and make light work of typing letters

AutoText

Word has the ability to greatly speed-up the entering of text you regularly use. In previous versions of Word this was known as a glossary, but in Word 6 it is called AutoText.

AutoCorrect of course (see previous pages) allows you to do this as an automatic — on-the-fly as-you-type — feature. If you don't want it to occur automatically but instead want manual control over automatic insertion of entries, use AutoText.

To use an AutoText entry in your documents, you first have to create it.

Basic steps:

CREATING AN ENTRY

1 Type in the text you want as an AutoText entry anywhere in a document. Select the text, then click the AutoText button on the Standard toolbar. This calls up the AutoText dialog box

2 Enter a new name for the entry (if the default name isn't suitable)

3 Click Add to accept the new entry

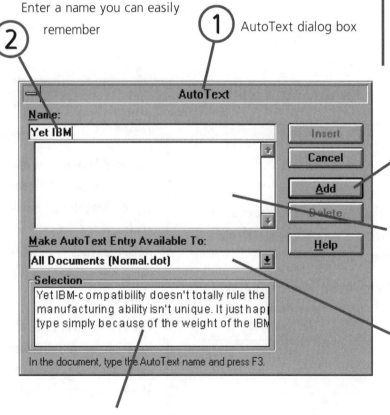

Enter a name you can easily remember

(2)

(1) AutoText dialog box

(3) Click to accept

List box of AutoText entries (currently empty, as this is the first AutoText entry)

You can specify the template the entry is available to (see page 136)

Preview of selected text

1 When you want to insert an AutoText entry into your document, type in the entry name you previously allocated

2 Click the AutoText button on the Standard toolbar or hit F3. The entry is inserted into the document

Once your entry is created, you can use it wherever and whenever you want in your documents.

When you want to insert an AutoText entry, simply type in the entry name...

> I shall give you these with my complements. Take them home and keep them. Add other complimentary things to them to make them whole.
> Yet IBM

...then click the AutoText button

②

> I shall give you these with my complements. Take them home and keep them. Add other complimentary things to them to make them whole.
> Yet IBM-compatibility doesn't totally rule the world. Its combination of hardware, software and manufacturing ability isn't unique. It just happened to create the biggest personal computer type simply because of the weight of the IBM name.

Tip:

As with AutoCorrect, the entries you create for AutoText can include graphical items and text formatting. Like AutoCorrect entries, too, you can use AutoText to insert boilerplate text into your documents.

In fact, the only *real* difference between AutoText and AutoCorrect as far as the ordinary user – you – is concerned is how the entries are inserted into your documents.

AutoCorrect entries are inserted automatically, as soon as the entry name is typed.

AutoText entries are inserted semi-automatically – *you* have to specify that the entry name be replaced with the entry.

They each have their uses

Outlining

We saw an outline view back on page 13. Outlining is another way of looking at your Word documents and, what's more important, is the best way of controlling how the various text parts within a document are organized and arranged.

Easiest way to see how outlining works is with an example. Let's say you've been working long and hard at a chapter of your book. It's a long chapter and technically quite involved — so involved that you're sure there's a problem somewhere, but you're not exactly sure *where*.

Basic steps:

1 Choose **View→Outline**, or type [Alt]+[V] then [O], or (best) click the Outline button [▤] at the lower-left corner of the document window. Your document is displayed in outline view

A document in outline view (1)

Microsoft Word - RTFTEXT.RTF

File Edit View Insert Format Tools Table Window Help

Heading 1 | Arial | 18 | **B** *I* U | ...

← ⇒ ⇨ | ⇧ ⇩ | ✛ — | 1 2 3 4 5 6 7 8 | All = ᴬ₄ 🗏

Outlining toolbar

- ▫ **Chapter 8**
- ✛ **Text in Zebadee**

Symbols

  - ▫ Zebadee is an electronic publishing program which allows you to define many aspects about each page to be published. Many operations to define these aspects are used so regularly that they really form the backbone of the program. It's critical, therefore, you understand these operations to get their best advantages.
  - ▫ One of the most basic of Zebadee's operations is the use of boxes on a page to define where each block of text (and each picture, for that matter) is positioned. While text boxes and picture boxes are handled by the user in a largely similar way, they are actually treated differently by the program and — of course — do different things.
  - ▫ So to all intents and purposes you should appreciate that there are two kinds of boxes: text boxes and picture boxes. Knowing how to define, adjust and manipulate each is vital. Here we deal with text boxes.

- ✛ **Defining a text box**

  - ▫ Text boxes are initially defined by drawing the box on a page (or pasteboard) using the mouse. Later, they can be adjusted using the mouse or by entering specific details in a dialog box or palette.
  - ▫ To define a text box first select the text box tool G. Note that the pointer becomes a small cross-hair pointer +, anywhere within the page's pasteboard boundary. Position the cross-hair pointer + at a corner of the area you wish to be allocated as a text box — it doesn't matter which corner.

Page 1 | Sec 1 | 1/36 | At 2.9cm | Ln 1 | Col 1 | 09:56 | REC | MRK | EXT | OVR | WP

Outline symbols

In outline view, your document is displayed with its headings and body text displayed with various symbols to their left. The symbols indicate what is associated with the various parts of a document.

Plus symbol indicates that a heading has either (or both) subheadings and body text beneath it

Minus symbol indicates that a heading has neither subheadings nor text beneath it

Box symbol indicates that text is body text (that is, it's not a heading of any kind)

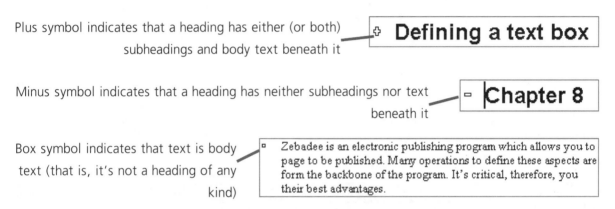

Outlining toolbar

Along with outline view comes the Outlining toolbar, with its new buttons

Moves a heading up

Expand subheadings and body text under a heading

Expand or collapse the outline to the required number of levels

Master document view

Promotes a heading to a higher level

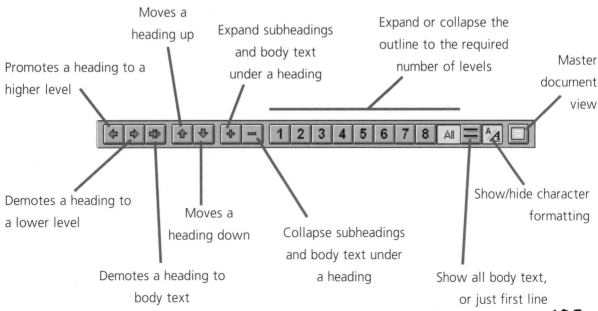

Demotes a heading to a lower level

Moves a heading down

Collapse subheadings and body text under a heading

Show/hide character formatting

Demotes a heading to body text

Show all body text, or just first line

Outlining (contd)

In essence, outlining allows you to:

● get an overall view of your document — to various degrees of complexity

● easily move headings around (while their associated subheadings and body text parts move automatically with them).

Another example can show you.

1 Click the Show/hide character formatting button and the Expand/collapse to level 1 button on the Outlining toolbar.

Now all character formatting has gone, and only the first level headings are displayed

① Document with character formatting hidden and levels collapsed to level 1

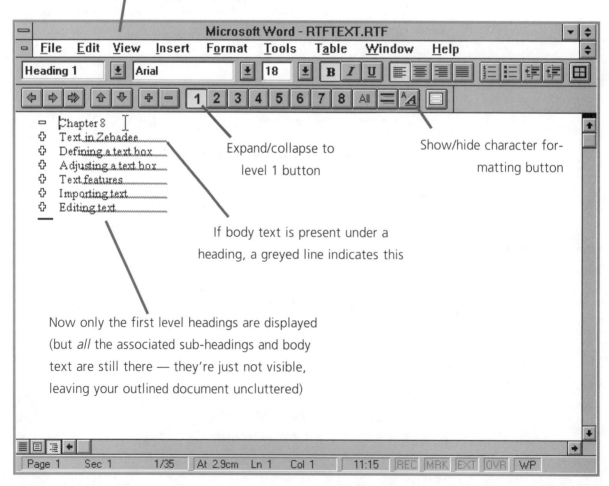

Expand/collapse to level 1 button

Show/hide character formatting button

If body text is present under a heading, a greyed line indicates this

Now only the first level headings are displayed (but *all* the associated sub-headings and body text are still there — they're just not visible, leaving your outlined document uncluttered)

2 Select the headings *Defining a text box*, and *Adjusting a text box*. Now click the Demote heading button  on the Outlining toolbar

3 Select the heading *Editing text*, then click the Move heading up button

From this position, let's now say you realise that:

● the level 1 headings *Defining a text box*, and *Adjusting a text box* really *should* be level 2 headings

● the heading *Editing text* should be before the heading *Importing text*.

With outlining, that's easily done.

Headings demoted to next level down ②

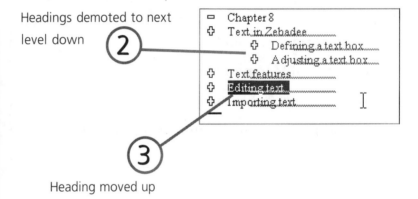

③

Heading moved up

Tables

Earlier in the book we saw how to produce a simple table using tab stops. This is fine for just that — simple tables — but for anything more complex than just a couple of rows and columns things can be made much easier with Word's in-built table feature.

Tables are made up by a collection of *cells*, in rows and columns. Word displays a table in *gridlines* (dotted lines around all the cells of a table) which are not printed and are merely provided on-screen for guidance.

You can add text or graphical elements to cells of a Word table, and you can format text in any character or paragraph format as usual.

You create a table in one of two ways:

● from the Insert Table dialog box

● with the Table button on the Standard toolbar.

Basic steps:

INSERT TABLE DIALOG BOX

1 Position the insertion point where you want to create a table, then choose **Table⊣Insert Table**, or type ⌷Alt⌷+⌷A⌷ then ⌷I⌷. This calls up the Insert Table dialog box

2 Enter the numbers of columns and rows you want

3 Click OK to create the table — Word displays the empty table as dotted gridlines

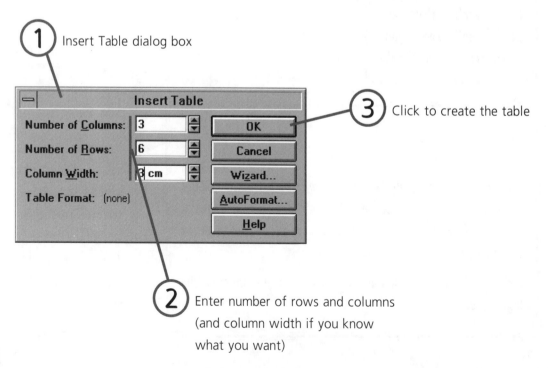

1 Insert Table dialog box

3 Click to create the table

2 Enter number of rows and columns (and column width if you know what you want)

INSERT TABLE BUTTON

1 Position the insertion point
where you want to create
a table, then click the
Insert Table button 🈸 on
the Standard toolbar

2 Drag across the drop-down
grid to select the number
of columns and rows you
want, then let go the
mouse button

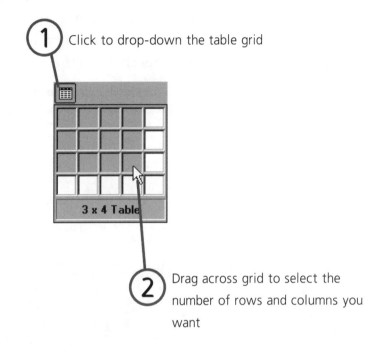

① Click to drop-down the table grid

② Drag across grid to select the
number of rows and columns you
want

The insertion point is positioned at the top-left cell in
the table ready for you to enter text. You move around
in a table by clicking the mouse in another cell, tabbing
with the [Tab] key, or pressing the [↑][↓][←][→] keys in the
direction you want to move.

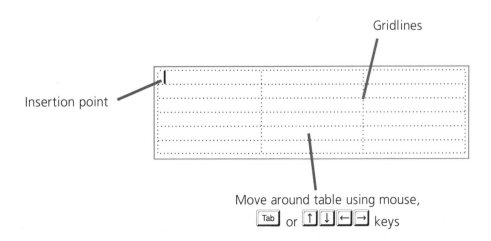

Gridlines

Insertion point

Move around table using mouse,
[Tab] or [↑][↓][←][→] keys

Tables (contd)

Once you've created a table you can change it to suit. You can drag column widths and indents from the document ruler (bottom) and you can drag a column gridline left or right to suit directly from the table.

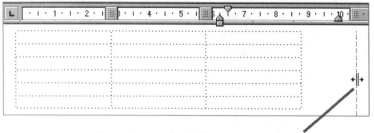

Dragging end gridline out to enlarge column

 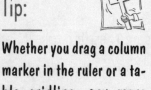
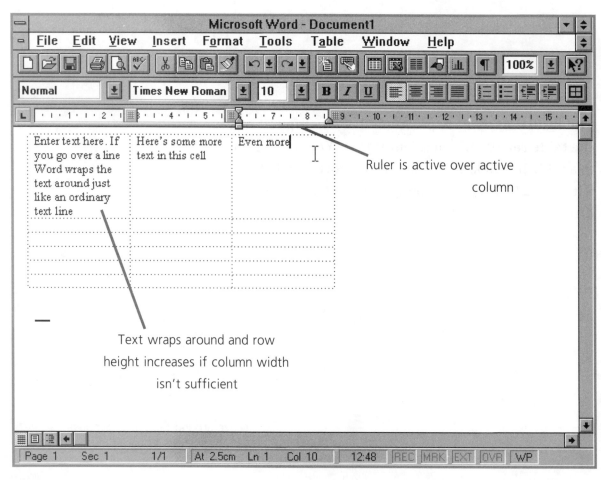

Ruler is active over active column

Text wraps around and row height increases if column width isn't sufficient

Table conversions

Even if you've already entered text you can still convert it into a Word table. Simply make sure there are separators which Word recognises — commas or tabs between the items of text you want in each cell, and paragraph marks between each row — in the text.

Basic steps:

1 Select the text you want to convert to a table

2 Click the Insert Table button 🖽 on the Standard toolbar — that text is converted into a table

Select the text you want to convert into a table
— make sure it has adequate separators ①

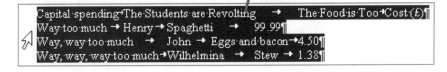

Capital spending¤	The Students are Revolting¤	The Food is Too¤	Cost (£)¤
Way too much¤	Henry¤	Spaghetti¤	99.99¤
Way, way too much¤	John¤	Eggs and bacon¤	4.50¤
Way, way, way too much¤	Wilhelmina¤	Stew¤	1.38¤

② Converted into a table

Take note:

You can convert a table into text, too, in a similar way. First select the rows you want to convert into text then choose **Table⊦Convert Table to Text**. Then, in the Convert Table to Text dialog box, choose the character you want to separate text with, and finally click **OK**

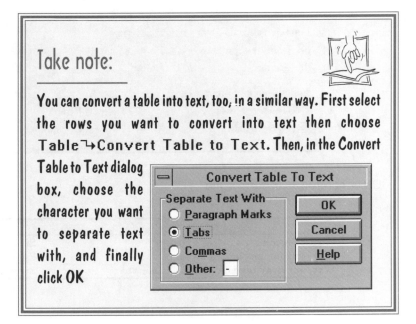

111

Table formatting

Once you've created a table, you can format it in all the usual ways. However, Word gives you several suggested options to format it automatically, which are both faster and (probably) better than doing it manually.

Basic steps:

1 Select the table and choose **Table→Table AutoFormat**, or type `Alt`+`A` then `F`, to call up the Table AutoFormat dialog box

2 From the list of formats select one you want

3 Click OK to accept format onto your table

① Table AutoFormat dialog box

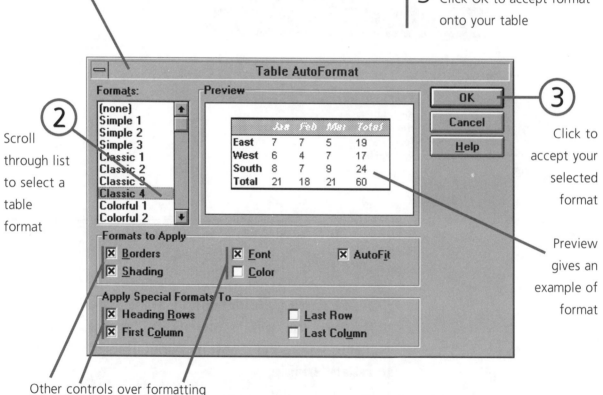

Scroll through list to select a table format

② Other controls over formatting

③ Click to accept your selected format

Preview gives an example of format

The table on the previous page, formatted with the Classic 4 format above

Counting your words

When all your text has been entered into a document, it's often necessary to count the total number of words in it. Most publishers need a word count, for example, to give some idea of how long a document is, therefore a rough estimate of how many pages it'll fill in the finished publication.

Word can do much more than just count the words in a document, however.

1 Choose **Tools ⤷ Word Count**, or type Alt + T then W, to call up the Word Count dialog box

① Word Count dialog box

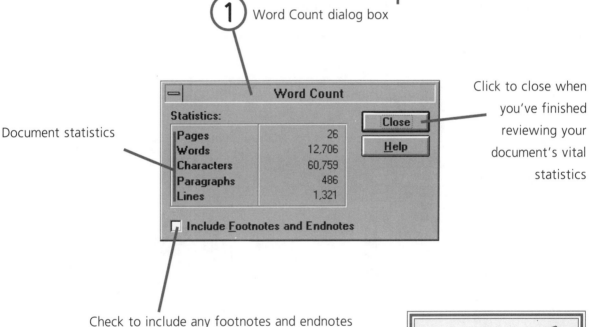

Document statistics

Click to close when you've finished reviewing your document's vital statistics

Check to include any footnotes and endnotes in the word count

Tip:

If you need to do a word count often, it's probably better to assign a keyboard shortcut to the Word Count command. See page 147 for details of assigning shortcut keys

Tip:

If you select text prior to calling up the Word Count dialog box, only the selected text (pages, words, characters, paragraphs and lines) is included

Graphics

You can import a graphic created in another application into a Word document. Once imported, any graphic can be edited in several ways.

> ## Tip:
>
> You can also cut and paste a graphic into a Word document from another application (or indeed another Word document)

Basic steps:

IMPORTING A GRAPHIC

1 Position the insertion point where you want the graphic to be placed. Choose **Insert⇥Picture**, or type `Alt`+`I` then `P`

2 Locate the graphic you want in the Insert Picture dialog box and click OK. The graphic is imported to your document

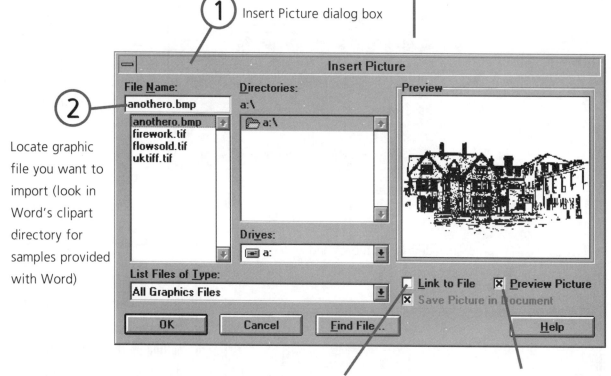

① Insert Picture dialog box

② Locate graphic file you want to import (look in Word's clipart directory for samples provided with Word)

You can create a link to a graphic file by checking here, such that the file itself is not imported (only its screen representation and details of the link). This keeps your Word document file size down, while Word refers to the link as it prints the document

Check to preview picture in box above

Basic steps:

EDITING A GRAPHIC

1 Click on a graphic

2 You can drag any of the box handles to adjust the size or shape

① Select a graphic by clicking on it

As you let go the mouse button, the graphic resizes itself

②

Drag a box handle to resize a graphic. Dragging a corner handle resizes the graphic proportionally. Dragging a middle handle resizes it disproportionally

Take note:

Word uses special files called graphics filters to let it import graphics files. While Windows bitmaps (with the extension *.bmp*). Windows metafiles (*.wmf*) and tag image file format files (*.tif*) are imported directly, you need filters (available from Microsoft) to import any other graphics file formats

Tip:

You can effectively box a graphic by creating a border around it using the Borders toolbar. Shading, too, can be used to a good effect (see page 60 for details of creating borders and shading)

Summary for Section 5

● Use Word's powerful find and replace commands to search for and change text or even just formatting withon your documents.

● Word's spelling checker can locate instances of mis-spelled words, but remember that a word mis-spelt in-context may still make a word spelled correctly out-of-context.

● Create custom dictionaries if you regularly use technical jargon.

● Word's on-line thesaurus can assist you in employing supplementary asseverations (OK — it finds new words!).

● Check your grammar to weed out those mis-spelled out-of-context words the spelling checker can't detect.

● Use AutoCorrect to correct spelling mistakes you regularly make, and automatically insert phrases at your abbreviated prompt.

● Use AutoText to insert phrases at your manual prompt.

● Remember that outlining helps you to organise your documents logically, and can be a boon when writing too.

● Tables in Word can be most effectively created with the Table command.

● You can import certain graphics files into your Word documents, then edit them in various ways.

6   Automatic formatting

Styles

Styles are the first method of automatic formatting. They are *extremely* important, because:

● their use makes it easy to define the formats which any particular paragraph has applied to it

● styles are groups of formats gathered together under one label (all the formats considered in Section 3 — and some others — can be gathered together and given just a single style name)

● if you apply a style to selected text *all* that text has the same formats applied to it simultaneously

● all you need to do to apply a style to selected text is choose that style from a drop-down list — the text is formatted with all the individual formats just by this one action

● you can define as many styles as you want for a document — one for each group of formats the document calls for.

You can use styles instantly, because any Word document has default styles already built in.

Basic steps:

1 Enter some text into a new Word document. Don't bother applying any character or paragraph formats yet. Make sure you type in a few paragraphs and make the top paragraph and some others single line ones — say headings or sub-headings

2 Select the top heading of the document (you can simply click anywhere in the first paragraph) then click the Style drop-down list box of the Formatting toolbar

② Select the top paragraph of the entered text — you don't need to select the *whole* paragraph, you only need to click *in* it

① Enter unformatted text into your document

Report into the oxidation of ferrous materials under load conditions
Oxidation defined
Under most circumstances, ferrous materials have iron in them. Iron is a substance which combines with oxygen under certain conditions, forming a chemical compound called an oxide.
Oxides are often of no concern — aluminium oxide for example is actually of some benefit in aluminium substances because it creates a hard barrier against physical damge to the rest of the material.
Ferrous oxide, on the other hand, *is* of concern. Ferrous oxide, aka iron oxide, aka rust is of particular importance because:
it looks grotty
it is weaker than its non-oxidised counterpart.
Load conditions
Under certain conditions ferrous oxidation occurs more rapidly than under other conditions. There are two critical conditions which, when applied together to ferrous materials, make the liklihood of oxidation much greater. These two conditions are:
application of moisture in the form of water or water vapour
application of oxygen in the form of gas.

3 From the Style drop-down list (a list of the default styles present in each new Word document) choose Heading 1

4 View the results of this style change

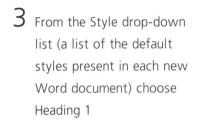

③ The Style drop-down list box. Defa styles for Word documents are list

Note how the whole paragraph has been formatted with the formats contained within the Heading 1 style

④ The style applied to the top paragraph — the document's heading

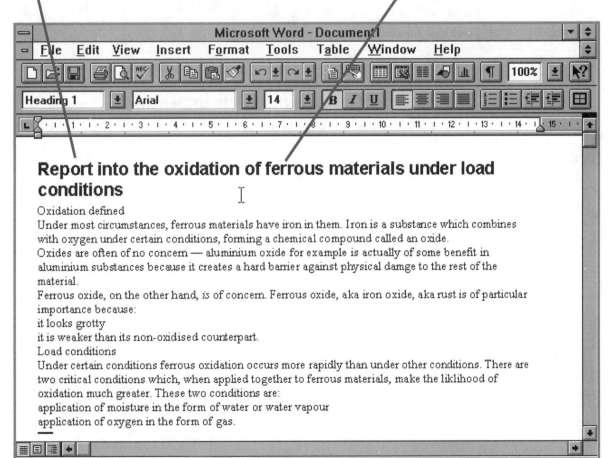

Report into the oxidation of ferrous materials under load conditions

Oxidation defined

Under most circumstances, ferrous materials have iron in them. Iron is a substance which combines with oxygen under certain conditions, forming a chemical compound called an oxide.

Oxides are often of no concern — aluminium oxide for example is actually of some benefit in aluminium substances because it creates a hard barrier against physical damge to the rest of the material.

Ferrous oxide, on the other hand, *is* of concern. Ferrous oxide, aka iron oxide, aka rust is of particular importance because:

it looks grotty

it is weaker than its non-oxidised counterpart.

Load conditions

Under certain conditions ferrous oxidation occurs more rapidly than under other conditions. There are two critical conditions which, when applied together to ferrous materials, make the liklihood of oxidation much greater. These two conditions are:

application of moisture in the form of water or water vapour

application of oxygen in the form of gas.

Styles (contd)

Basic steps:

5 Continue applying styles in
the same way, trying out
the other heading styles
available

(5) Apply other styles to your document in
the same way as before

Heading 1   Heading 2

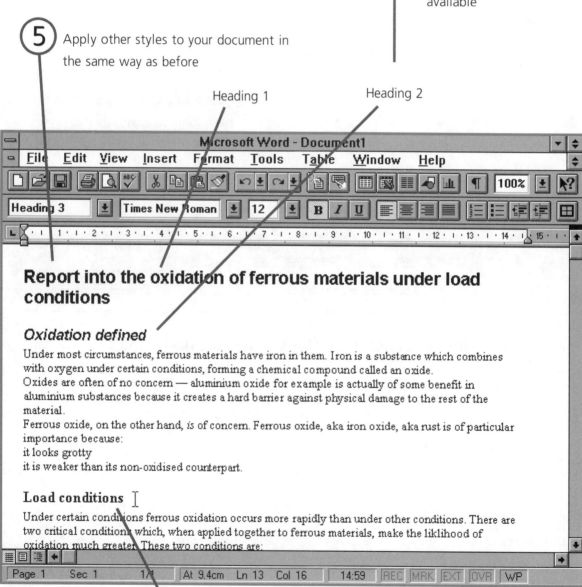

Heading 3

The screenshot shows Microsoft Word - Document1 with the text:

Report into the oxidation of ferrous materials under load conditions

Oxidation defined

Under most circumstances, ferrous materials have iron in them. Iron is a substance which combines with oxygen under certain conditions, forming a chemical compound called an oxide.

Oxides are often of no concern — aluminium oxide for example is actually of some benefit in aluminium substances because it creates a hard barrier against physical damage to the rest of the material.

Ferrous oxide, on the other hand, *is* of concern. Ferrous oxide, aka iron oxide, aka rust is of particular importance because:

it looks grotty

it is weaker than its non-oxidised counterpart.

Load conditions

Under certain conditions ferrous oxidation occurs more rapidly than under other conditions. There are two critical conditions which, when applied together to ferrous materials, make the liklihood of oxidation much greater. These two conditions are:

120

Character and paragraph styles

There are two types of styles:

● character styles

● paragraph styles.

They are identified by their appearance in the Styles drop-down list of the Formatting toolbar. They work in essentially the same way (that is, you select the text to be stylised, then select the style) but what they do to the selected text differs.

Character styles are displayed in a lighter font. When you apply a character style to selected text, only the selected text (that is, not the whole paragraph — unless the whole paragraph is selected!) has the formats applied

Normal	▼
Default Paragraph Font	
Heading 1	
Heading 2	
Heading 3	
Normal	

Paragraph styles are displayed in a heavier font. When you apply a paragraph font to selected text, the *whole* paragraph has the formats applied

---

Take note:

Styles are important for at least two reasons:

● **because they speed up the way you can format a document. Rather than formatting each selection of text with individual character and paragraph formats (which can take some time if you have quite a few formats to apply) you can apply *all* the formats in one operation**

● **because the formats you apply as a style are always the same, there is no chance that you have forgotten any particular formats — if you apply each format individually you will probably forget some of them — all text with a particular style applied is identical in formats**

Creating styles

There are three main ways you can create your own paragraph style:

● apply formats to your own sample text, until it is the way you want it, then create the style from those formats (for most people, this is ideal)

● adapt another style to suit

● copy styles from other documents to your own.

Basic steps:

1 To create a style from your own sample text, apply formats to your text until it is the way you want it (look again at Section 3 if you're a bit hazy about formatting)

2 Select the text you want to make a style of

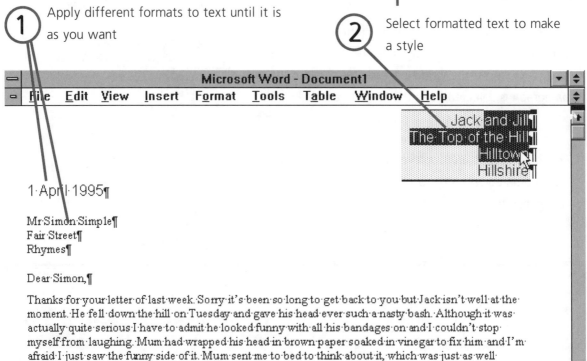

① Apply different formats to text until it is as you want

② Select formatted text to make a style

Microsoft Word - Document1

File   Edit   View   Insert   Format   Tools   Table   Window   Help

Jack and Jill¶
The Top of the Hill¶
Hilltown¶
Hillshire¶

1 April 1995¶

Mr Simon Simple¶
Fair Street¶
Rhymes¶

Dear Simon,¶

Thanks for your letter of last week. Sorry it's been so long to get back to you but Jack isn't well at the moment. He fell down the hill on Tuesday and gave his head ever such a nasty bash. Although it was actually quite serious I have to admit he looked funny with all his bandages on and I couldn't stop myself from laughing. Mum had wrapped his head in brown paper soaked in vinegar to fix him and I'm afraid I just saw the funny side of it. Mum sent me to bed to think about it, which was just as well because I was a bit bruised myself as I fell down after him.¶

We hope you managed to get something to eat when you went to the fair, but I hope you didn't ask the Pie man for a pie. You know how mean he is and won't give you anything for nothing.¶

Love from us both,¶

Jill (and Jack from his bed)¶

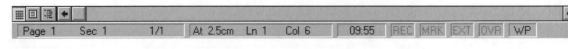

Page 1   Sec 1   1/1   At 2.5cm   Ln 1   Col 6   09:55   REC MRK EXT OVR WP

3 Choose **Format→Style**, or type [Alt]+[O] then [S], to call up the Style dialog box. Click New to call up the New Style dialog box

4 Enter a name for your style

5 Check the Add to Template check box, then click OK, then click Close in the Style dialog box

If you repeat this procedure for all the different styles within your document, when you have finished you will end up with a number of styles which have been added to Word (in the Normal template, actually), and which will be present whenever you open a new document following that template.

Next time you want to produce a similar looking document the styles are already there to use. Simply enter your text in the new document, select the text to be formatted with any particular style, then apply the style from the Formatting toolbar's Style button drop-down list. The text is formatted as you defined.

Click New in the Style dialog box

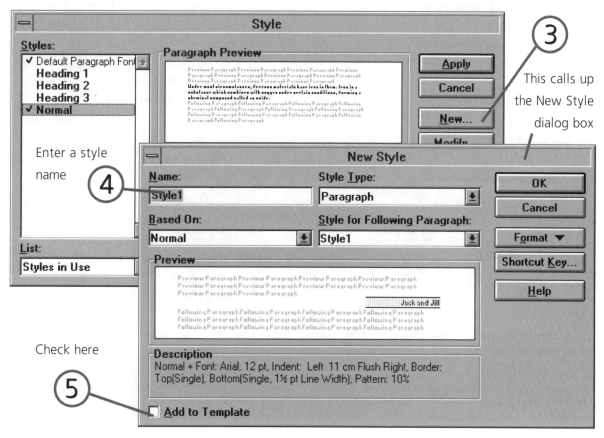

This calls up the New Style dialog box

Enter a style name

Check here

Creating styles (contd)

One of the beauties of styles is their ability to be modified. What's more, if you modify a style all text in a document which has been formatted with that style is modified too. This is extremely useful when you're formatting a document to appear how you want it, but also it's a useful method of creating your own styles.

Basic steps:

1 To modify a style choose **Format↳Style**, or type ⎇Alt + ⎗O then ⎚S, to call up the Style dialog box

2 Select the style you want to modify in the Styles entry liist, then click Modify to call up the Modify dialog box

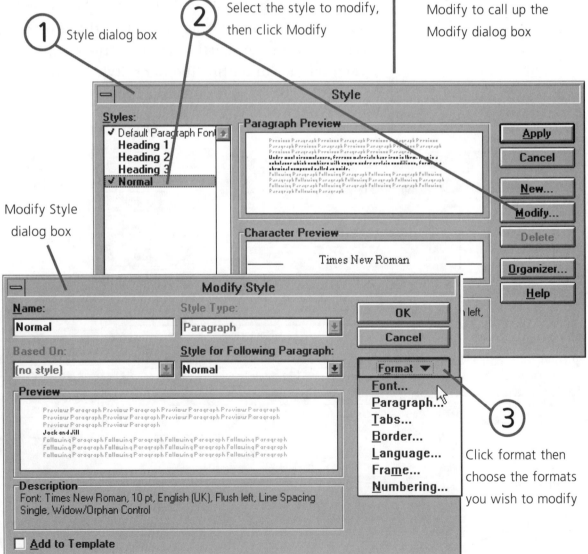

① Style dialog box

② Select the style to modify, then click Modify

Modify Style dialog box

③ Click format then choose the formats you wish to modify

124

3 Click the Format button to drop-down a list of formats which you can modify, select the format you want and in the resultant dialog box adjust formats to suit. Repeat this if you want to modify more than one format type

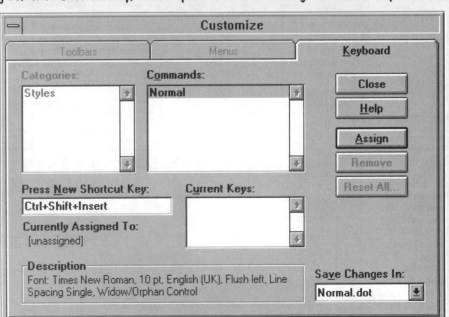

Creating styles (contd)

The last method of creating styles in a document is to copy styles from other documents which have the styles you want. It's the Organizer dialog box which allows you to do this, listing styles in two documents side-by-side, so that you can copy styles from one to the other.

The styles to be copied can be in a true Word document, or in a Word template. Word has many default templates which you can use for this purpose, and we'll use one to illustrate how you can do it.

1 To copy one or more styles from one document to another, choose **Format→Style**, or type `Alt`+`O` then `S`, to call up the Style dialog box. Click the Organizer button to call up the Organizer dialog box

(1) Organizer dialog box

Select
faxcover1.dot
in the list

(3)

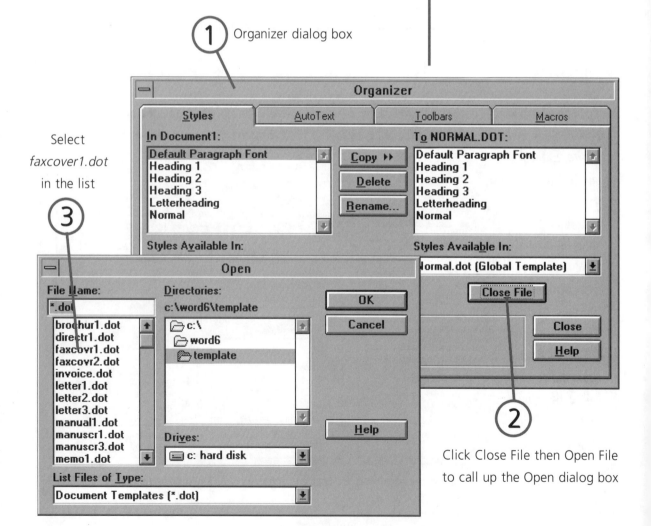

Click Close File then Open File to call up the Open dialog box

126

2 Click Close File on the *normal.dot* side of the dialog box (it changes to Open File) then click Open File. This displays a list of available files which you can select (if you haven't got the same list as shown, locate the templates directory in the Word directory on your hard disk and make sure you're listing files of **.dot* type)

3 Select *faxcover1.dot* in the list and click OK. Now the Organizer dialog box displays all the styles in the faxcover1 template in a scrollable list

4 You can select individual styles, or you can select multiple styles by [Ctrl] + clicking them. Copy them to your own document by clicking Copy

5 Click Close to close the Organizer dialog box, then try out your new styles in your own document

Select the styles you want in your own document

④

Organizer

| Styles | AutoText | Toolbars | Macros |

To Document1:

Default Paragraph Font
Heading 1
Heading 2
Heading 3
Letterheading
Normal

◄◄ Copy
Delete
Rename...

In FAXCOVR1.DOT:

Address
Annotation Reference
Annotation Text
Attention Line
Body Text
Body Text Indent
Body Text Keep

Styles Available In:

Document1 (Document)

Styles Available In:

Faxcovr1.dot (Template)

Close File

Close File

Description

Close
Help

Click close to try out the styles in your own document

⑤

127

More about styles

If you haven't already realised it, styles are very important to a word processor like Word. Styles form the key to producing professional documents with total consistency of formatting. Their use ensures efficient control over your documents.

However, there's a few additional things to know about styles which can make their use even more efficient. They are presented here as a collection ot tips and notes — bear them in mind when you use Word.

Tip:

When you create a new document, base it on a template — templates are complete with their own styles which you can use immediately. If there's a particular style of document you want, design it then save it as a template. Each time you create a new document based on that template it'll be exactly as you want it. (Templates are covered later.)

Tip:

Format all text in a document with styles — that way if you want to change the document's appearance you only have to change a handful of styles, not the various text elements

Tip:

While we've said all along how you should enter all your text first, then apply styles to it there is a more elegant way which calls on Word styles' ability to change to another style when a paragraph ends. In either the New Style or the Modify Style dialog boxes there is a drop-down list box called Style for Following Paragraph. In here is a list of all available styles. Choose one. Then as your style which has a specified style to follow ends, the next style comes into force.

This is useful, say, for headings and sub-headings (which are nearly always of a single paragraph and are followed by, say. normal style). As you finish typing the heading text and press ⏎ or Enter , the next paragraph is automatically stylised with the next style

Tip:

You can arrange your document window to display which style is applied to a paragraph (see below) by adjusting the **Style Area Width** box in the **View** tab of the **Options** dialog box (choose **Tools→Options**, or type `Alt`+`T` then `O`, then click **View** if it's not already at the front of the dialog box). Specify a width greater than 0 to display the style area in your document.

Take note:

If you delete a style (using, say, the Delete button on the Style dialog box) the Normal style is applied to all text which was formatted with the style

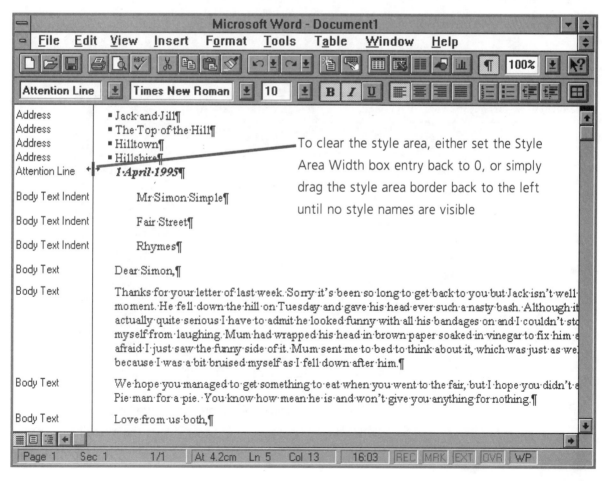

To clear the style area, either set the Style Area Width box entry back to 0, or simply drag the style area border back to the left until no style names are visible

More about styles (contd)

Check this to make sure a heading stays with its following text, without being left at the bottom of a page

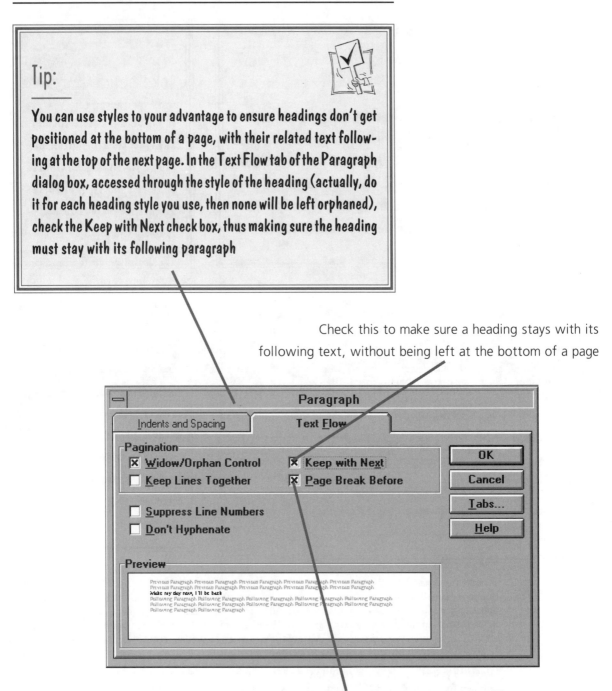

Check this to create a page break before a major heading — in other words the major heading will always start at the top of a page

130

Take note:

If you change a font, or any other formatting parameter, in a style which another style is based on, the other style's font (or other parameter) changes too – unless you have already specified a different parameter in the second style

Tip:

You can use the above to advantage when you set up the styles in your document – to specify the style which will follow another style. For example, if you specify that a heading is followed by body text then, every time you type a heading and press [Enter] or ⏎ (as long as Word knows that the heading *is* a heading – see next paragraph), the next paragraph will be in the body text style.

To enter styles as you go along, you *can* select the style from the style list box in the Formatting toolbar, but it's a lot easier to assign the style a keyboard shortcut which you can enter whenever you want to change style

Tip:

If you can't be bothered to arrange styles to best suit your documents, at least use Word's AutoFormat command (see over). This does a largely similar job, automatically. (Properly defines styles are always better, on the other hand)

Take note:

Styles are probably the most important feature of a word processor like Word. If you manage the styles in your documents properly, taking care in how they are formatted, how they are based, what text flow is associated with them and so on, your documents will be much better for it. Not only do they look *better*, but it is also much easier to make large formatting changes to suit the way you want your documents to look. For example, if all styles are based properly on each other in a hierarchical way a single change of font or size will change the whole document

AutoFormatting

While styles undoubtedly form a brilliant method of organising text and its appearance in your documents, Word's AutoFormat command takes the style approach one stage further — creating a method whereby a large number of styles can be applied to your document in one fell swoop.

Basic steps:

1 Enter text into a new document — don't bother creating, modifying or applying any styles

2 Commence automatic formatting by choosing **Format↳AutoFormat**, or type [Alt]+[O] then [A], to call up the AutoFormat dialog box

3 Click OK

① Enter your text with no styles applied

Chapter 11: Time is never long enough¶
After the bomb fell, people left didn't really feel like fighting anymore. They scurried around, scavenging what they could of food and clothes, knowing that Winter would be soon approaching. Wrapping its cold and icy fingers around their lives like beach towels after a swim in the open sea.¶
Whenever a battery could be located from what remained of shops and offices, it would be surreptitiously pocketed and carried home — in almost triumph — to be inserted into a household's transistor radio to scan the airwaves that night looking for outside survivors. The BBC World Service was the first station to begin broadcasting again. Once that was up and running everyone felt a little better, although it held no real candle in the night which was to soon engulf us.¶
People began to dig soil, turning over what used to be lawns, sowing seeds and tending seedlings with a care unpresent for many generations. It was a sight for sore eyes to venture into suburbia where mini-allotments grew up almost overnight, as stockbrokers, nurses, teachers and bankers alike turned their attentions to the earth. As it became apparent it wasn't just their town, their city, their country or their continent to be affected by the bomb, it seemed to be the only way forward. Dig for victory — ha! Dig for your bloody life is all¶

② AutoFormat dialog box

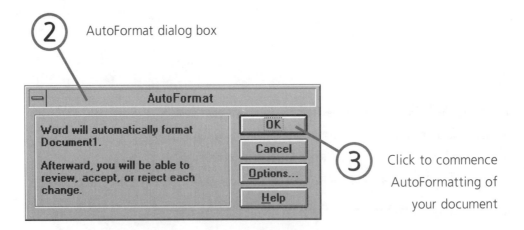

③ Click to commence AutoFormatting of your document

132

AutoFormat dialog box changes
to inform you of progress

4 The document is formatted
automatically with styles
throughout and the
AutoFormat dialog box
informs you of this when it
is done

5 Clicking the Review
Changes button to call up
the Review AutoFormat
Changes dialog box

AutoFormat

Formatting completed. You can now:
- **Accept or reject all changes.**
- **Review and reject individual changes.**
- **Choose a custom look with Style Gallery.**

Accept
Reject All
Help

Review **C**hanges...   **S**tyle Gallery...

Step through changes made and reject any you don't want.
Close the dialog box (if you have made rejections) or Cancel
it (if you haven't) to get back to the AutoFormat dialog box

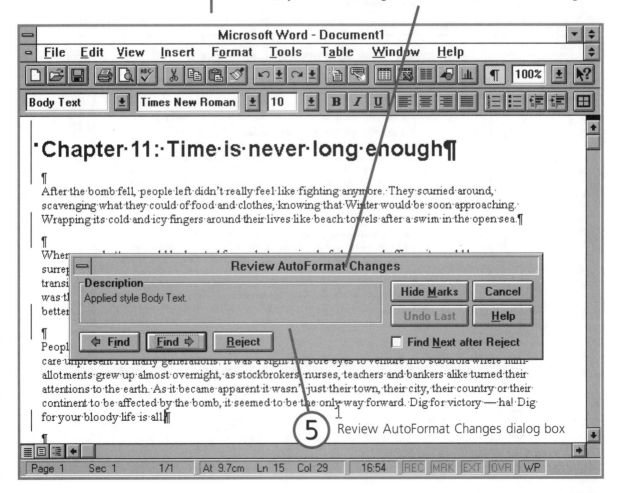

Microsoft Word - Document1

File   **Edit**   **View**   **Insert**   **Format**   **Tools**   **Table**   **Window**   **Help**

Body Text   Times New Roman   10   **B** *I* U

·Chapter·11:·Time·is·never·long·enough¶

¶
After·the·bomb·fell,·people·left·didn't·really·feel·like·fighting·anymore.·They·scurried·around,·
scavenging·what·they·could·of·food·and·clothes,·knowing·that·Winter·would·be·soon·approaching.·
Wrapping·its·cold·and·icy·fingers·around·their·lives·like·beach·towels·after·a·swim·in·the·open·sea.¶

¶
When...

Review AutoFormat Changes

Description
Applied style Body Text.

Hide **M**arks   Cancel

Undo Last   Help

⇐ **F**ind   **F**ind ⇒   **R**eject   ☐ Find **N**ext after Reject

Peopl...
care·unpresent·for·many·generations.·It·was·a·sight·for·sore·eyes·to·venture·into·suburbia·where·mini-
allotments·grew·up·almost·overnight,·as·stockbrokers,·nurses,·teachers·and·bankers·alike·turned·their·
attentions·to·the·earth.·As·it·became·apparent·it·wasn't·just·their·town,·their·city,·their·country·or·their·
continent·to·be·affected·by·the·bomb,·it·seemed·to·be·the·only·way·forward.·Dig·for·victory — ha!·Dig·
for·your·bloody·life·is·all¶

5 Review AutoFormat Changes dialog box

Page 1   Sec 1   1/1   At 9.7cm   Ln 15   Col 29   16:54   REC MRK EXT OVR WP

AutoFormatting (contd)

6 Now click the Style Gallery button. This calls up the Style Gallery dialog box

7 Click OK to accept a template, and click Accept in the AutoFormat dialog box to return to the fully formatted document to review your work

Select a template to be used as your document's AutoFormat style

Style Gallery dialog box

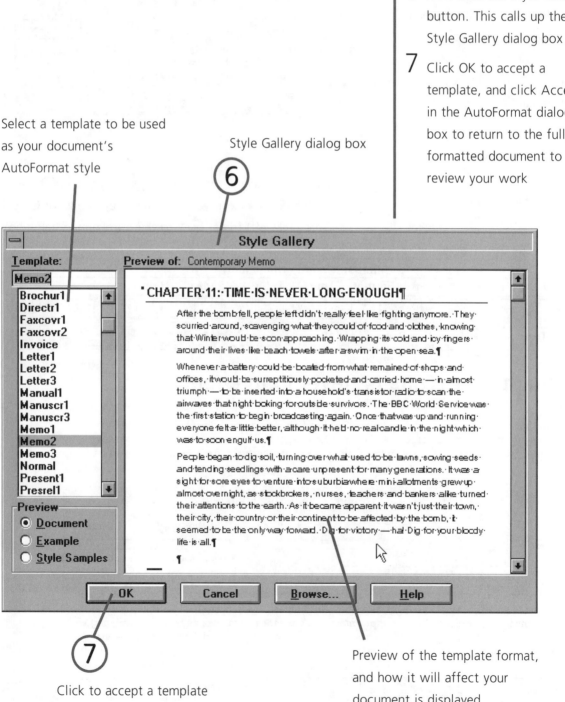

Style Gallery

Template:

Memo2

- Brochur1
- Directr1
- Faxcovr1
- Faxcovr2
- Invoice
- Letter1
- Letter2
- Letter3
- Manual1
- Manuscr1
- Manuscr3
- Memo1
- **Memo2**
- Memo3
- Normal
- Present1
- Presrel1

Preview of: Contemporary Memo

CHAPTER·11:·TIME·IS·NEVER·LONG·ENOUGH¶

After·the·bomb·fell,·people·left·didn't·really·feel·like·fighting·anymore.·They·scurried·around,·scavenging·what·they·could·of·food·and·clothes,·knowing·that·Winter·would·be·soon·approaching.·Wrapping·its·cold·and·icy·fingers·around·their·lives·like·beach·towels·after·a·swim·in·the·open·sea.¶

Whenever·a·battery·could·be·located·from·what·remained·of·shops·and·offices,·it·would·be·surreptitiously·pocketed·and·carried·home·—·in·almost·triumph·—·to·be·inserted·into·a·household's·transistor·radio·to·scan·the·airwaves·that·night·looking·for·outside·survivors.·The·BBC·World·Service·was·the·first·station·to·begin·broadcasting·again.·Once·that·was·up·and·running·everyone·felt·a·little·better,·although·it·held·no·real·candle·in·the·night·which·was·to·soon·engulf·us.¶

People·began·to·dig·soil,·turning·over·what·used·to·be·lawns,·sowing·seeds·and·tending·seedlings·with·a·care·unpresent·for·many·generations.·It·was·a·sight·for·sore·eyes·to·venture·into·suburbia·where·mini·allotments·grew·up·almost·overnight,·as·stockbrokers,·nurses,·teachers·and·bankers·alike·turned·their·attentions·to·the·earth.·As·it·became·apparent·it·wasn't·just·their·town,·their·city,·their·country·or·their·continent·to·be·affected·by·the·bomb,·it·seemed·to·be·the·only·way·forward.·Dig·for·victory·—·ha!·Dig·for·your·bloody·life·is·all.¶

¶

Preview
- ● **Document**
- ○ **Example**
- ○ **Style Samples**

[OK] [Cancel] [Browse...] [Help]

7 Click to accept a template

Preview of the template format, and how it will affect your document is displayed

AutoFormat options

While Word happily AutoFormats documents for you in the way described, and there doesn't seem to be much you can do about it, you *do* actually have considerable control over how Word does the job. What's more, you can use the options available to your advantage doing certain word processing tasks.

Basic steps:

1 Choose **Tools⤳Options**, or type ⌨Alt+⌨T then ⌨O, to call up the Options dialog box

2 Click the AutoFormat tab. This displays the AutoFormat options which you can adjust

Options dialog box ①

The AutoFormat options tab ②

If this box is checked, AutoFormat only applies styles automatically to unstyled text (that is, text with Normal or Body Text styles). In other words, if *you* apply a style to text it won't be changed

Select which text elements you want AutoFormatting to apply styles to here

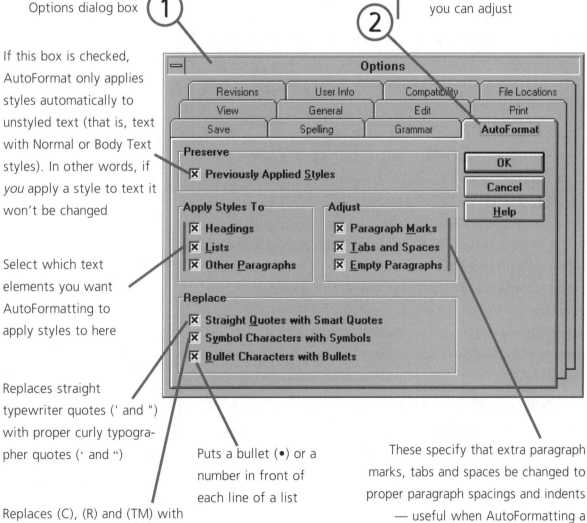

Replaces straight typewriter quotes (' and ") with proper curly typographer quotes (' and ")

Puts a bullet (•) or a number in front of each line of a list

These specify that extra paragraph marks, tabs and spaces be changed to proper paragraph spacings and indents — useful when AutoFormatting a document entered using *typist* rather than *word processor* typing methods

Replaces (C), (R) and (TM) with ©, ® and ™

135

About templates

In places throughout the book, the term *template* has been used, without any clear explanation. Now it's time to say exactly *what* a template is.

Effectively, a template is a skeleton document. It has all the bones of any document, in terms of document parameters — just not all the flesh in terms of text you enter.

Word (version 6 onwards, at least) uses templates to store all document parameters. Character and paragraph formats, tables, styles, sections, AutoText entries, graphical items and so on — and even text — can all be stored in a template.

Then, when you create a new document, you can base it on the chosen template and up pops a new document looking exactly as you want it — all you need to do is enter any final details and *hey, presto!,* a complete document. You could use a template, for example, when you create a letter. In the template might be a letterhead, complete with a company logo, and styles which specify fonts and formats for use in the letter. Another example could be a template setup for your monthly sales figures — the document is complete; you just add the figures. See over for details of creating your own template.

A default installation of Word includes a number of built-in templates as standard. When you first startup Word, the first document on-screen is even based on a template (the Normal template, actually). When you create a *new* document, on the other hand, you are given an option to choose which of the built-in templates you want to use for the document.

Basic steps:

1 Choose **File➔New**, or type [Alt]+[F] then [N], or type [Ctrl]+[N]. This calls up the New dialog box

2 Scroll through the template list box to see the templates available to you

3 Click on the template you want to select (default is Normal)

4 Click OK to create the document based on that template

Tip:

You can bypass the New dialog box if you want to create a document speedily. Just click the New button 🗋 on the Standard toolbar and a new document — based on the Normal template — is automatically created

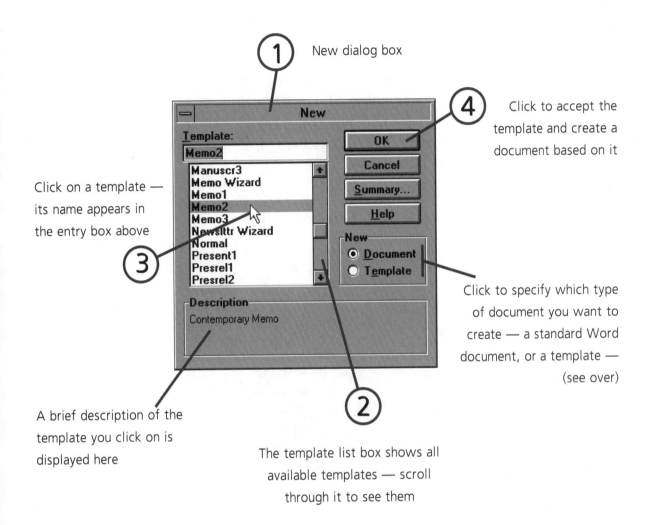

① New dialog box

④ Click to accept the template and create a document based on it

Click on a template — its name appears in the entry box above

③

A brief description of the template you click on is displayed here

② The template list box shows all available templates — scroll through it to see them

Click to specify which type of document you want to create — a standard Word document, or a template — (see over)

Take note:

The Normal template is a special case template – it holds all the document parameters you use most in Word. All the toolbars, their buttons, their positions, the menus and shortcut keys, and everything else you have as default items, are stored in the Normal template. If you use another template to create other documents, on the other hand, all these features are still available in those other documents

Creating a template

It's easy to create your own template. If there's a document type you find you're using quite a lot, it's worth making a template of it, then whenever you want to create another document with the same style just create the document from the template.

Once you've got the document looking just the way you want it (remember, you only need the bare bones of it), follow the steps here.

Basic steps:

1 Choose **File ↳ Save As**, or type [Alt] + [F] then [A]. This calls up the Save As dialog box

2 Click the Save File as Type drop-down list box to see the drop-down list of types you can save the document as

3 Select Document Template

4 Enter a name for your template — something easy to remember

5 Click OK

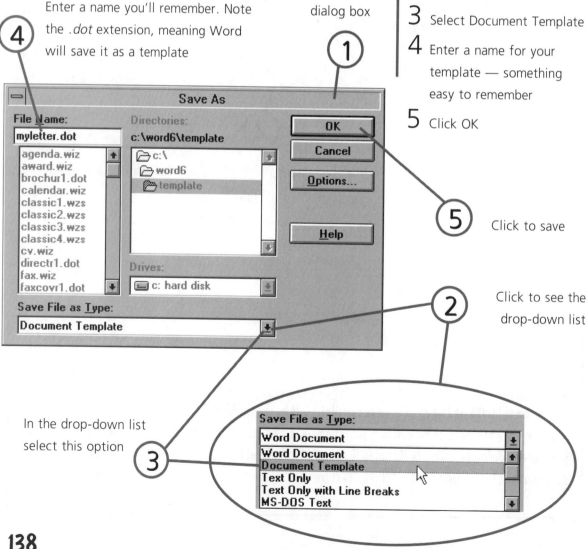

4 Enter a name you'll remember. Note the *.dot* extension, meaning Word will save it as a template

Save As dialog box

1

Save As

File Name:
myletter.dot

Directories:
c:\word6\template

agenda.wiz
award.wiz
brochur1.dot
calendar.wiz
classic1.wzs
classic2.wzs
classic3.wzs
classic4.wzs
cv.wiz
directr1.dot
fax.wiz
faxcovr1.dot

🗀 c:\
🗀 word6
🗀 template

Drives:
🖴 c: hard disk

OK
Cancel
Options...
Help

5 Click to save

2 Click to see the drop-down list

Save File as Type:
Document Template

In the drop-down list select this option

3

Save File as Type:
Word Document

Word Document
Document Template
Text Only
Text Only with Line Breaks
MS-DOS Text

138

Here's an example of a template for a letterhead. It combines a heading with a border (the underlining) and a simple graphic

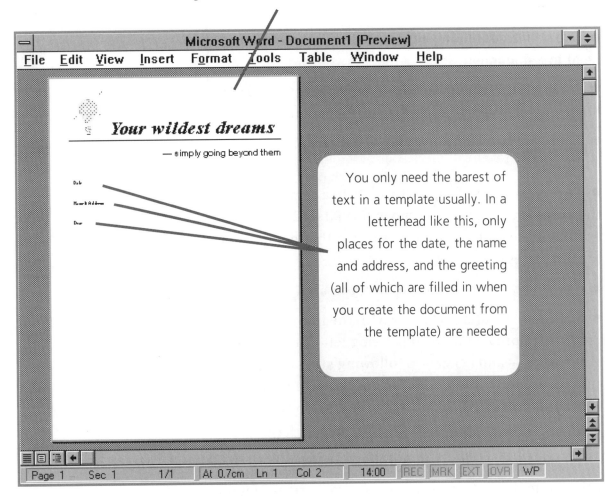

You only need the barest of text in a template usually. In a letterhead like this, only places for the date, the name and address, and the greeting (all of which are filled in when you create the document from the template) are needed

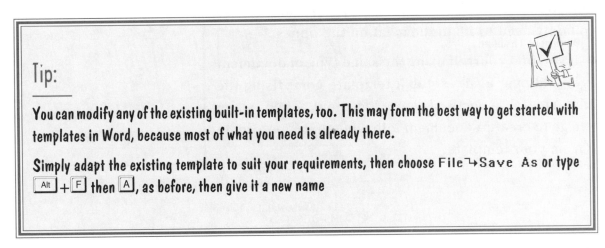

Tip:

You can modify any of the existing built-in templates, too. This may form the best way to get started with templates in Word, because most of what you need is already there.

Simply adapt the existing template to suit your requirements, then choose File⤷Save As or type `Alt` + `F` then `A`, as before, then give it a new name

139

Summary for Section 6

- Use styles containing all formatting parameters you need in a document.

- Setup styles which are based on other styles. Use a hierarchy of styles to create your document.

- There are two kinds of styles — paragraph and character styles.

- To create styles (1) apply formats to a sample of text then create the style from those formats, (2) adapt an existing style, or (3) copy styles from other documents (or templates).

- Use keyboard shortcuts to help you apply styles.

- Make sure headings (1) stay with the following paragraph — to prevent a heading being left at the bottom of the page — and (2) have a following style — to make sure your body style, say, is automatically applied when you press Enter or ⏎. Use styles to do this.

- If you can't be bothered — or don't know how — to setup your own styles, use AutoFormatting.

- Use templates to speed up how you create good-looking documents. Templates hold skeleton information about a document — styles, graphics, some text — you only need to fill in the meat on the bones.

- If you find yourself using the same type of document over and over again, setup a template comprising the fundamental aspects of your document. Then, when you go to create a document following that type, create it from your template.

7 Technical thingamajigs

Print preview

Before you print a document, it's best to stand back and take a look at it. Print previewing does this job for you, giving you an overall view of the document before you go ahead and waste your paper while letting you edit the document if you need.

Print preview brings with it its own toolbar, with some new buttons.

1 Choose **File→Print Preview**, or type `Alt`+`F` then `V`, or simply (best) click the Print Preview button on the Standard toolbar. The display changes to print preview, fitting complete pages of your document into the print preview window

2 Use buttons on the Print Preview toolbar to adjust the display to suit

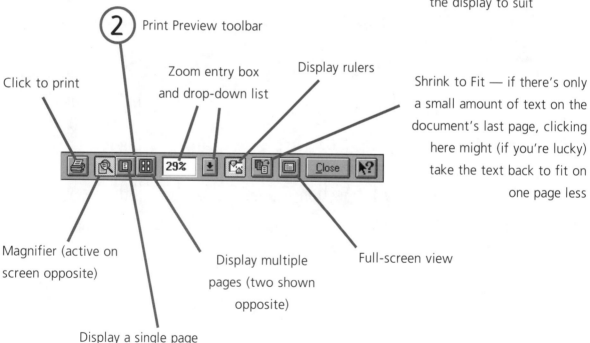

(2) Print Preview toolbar

Click to print

Zoom entry box and drop-down list

Display rulers

Shrink to Fit — if there's only a small amount of text on the document's last page, clicking here might (if you're lucky) take the text back to fit on one page less

Magnifier (active on screen opposite)

Display multiple pages (two shown opposite)

Full-screen view

Display a single page

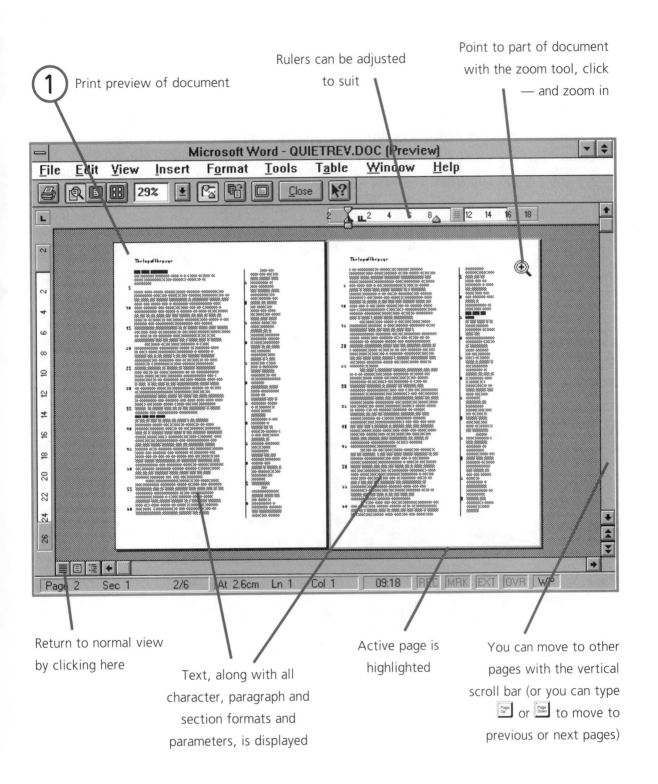

(1) Print preview of document

Rulers can be adjusted to suit

Point to part of document with the zoom tool, click — and zoom in

Microsoft Word - QUIETREV.DOC (Preview)

File   Edit   View   Insert   Format   Tools   Table   Window   Help

29%   Close

Page 2   Sec 1   2/6   At 2.6cm   Ln 1   Col 1   09:18   REC   MRK   EXT   OVR   WP

Return to normal view by clicking here

Text, along with all character, paragraph and section formats and parameters, is displayed

Active page is highlighted

You can move to other pages with the vertical scroll bar (or you can type Page Up or Page Down to move to previous or next pages)

143

Printing

While printing from a PC can give many headaches, use of the Windows environment coupled with Word itself makes life a lot easier. We have, however, to assume that your computer is properly connected to a printer, and that both are on and working. After that, there are only a few things you need to know.

Basic steps:

1 Choose **File→Print**, or type `Alt`+`F` then `P`, or type `Ctrl`+`P`. This calls up the Print dialog box

2 As the default dialog box stands, if you click OK, one copy of the text in the active document will be printed to the printer shown — you can adjust controls and entries to change this

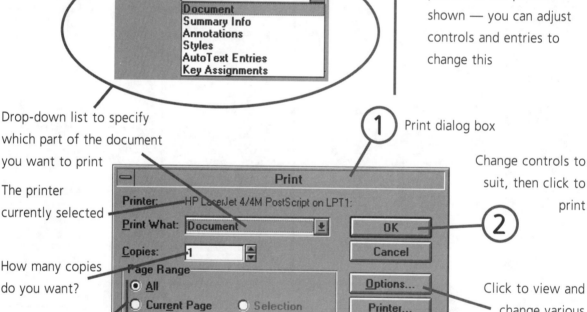

Drop-down list to specify which part of the document you want to print

The printer currently selected

How many copies do you want?

Specify which pages you want to print

Drop-down list allows you to print both sides, or specified sides of double-sided documents

Print dialog box

Change controls to suit, then click to print

Click to view and change various printing options (see opposite)

Click to change printer

Print options

Apart from controlling print parameters such as number of copies, which pages and so on, you can specify other, more technical, things too. Important ones are shown below.

Tip:

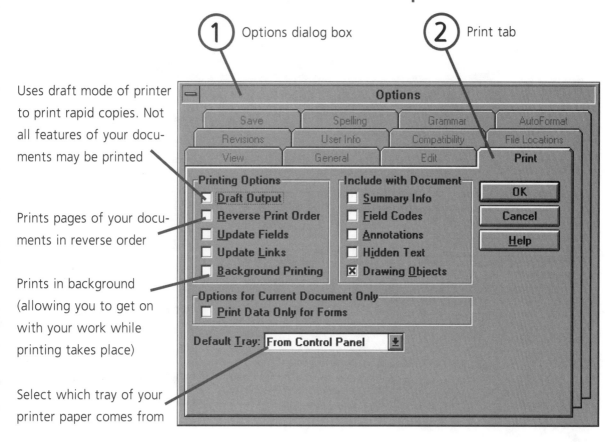

You can speed up the printing process by simply clicking the Print button 🖨 on the Standard toolbar. This bypasses the Print dialog box altogether and prints the document with default settings – for most printing purposes this is fine

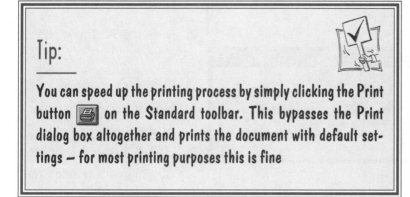

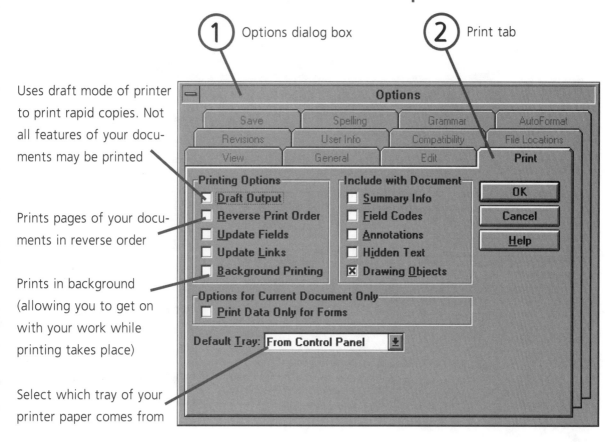

Basic steps:

1 From the Print dialog box, click Options. This calls up the Options dialog box

2 Click the Print tab, if it's not already frontmost

(1) Options dialog box

(2) Print tab

Uses draft mode of printer to print rapid copies. Not all features of your documents may be printed

Prints pages of your documents in reverse order

Prints in background (allowing you to get on with your work while printing takes place)

Select which tray of your printer paper comes from

Options

Save	Spelling	Grammar	AutoFormat
Revisions	User Info	Compatibility	File Locations
View	General	Edit	Print

Printing Options
- ◉ Draft Output
- ☐ Reverse Print Order
- ☐ Update Fields
- ☐ Update Links
- ☐ Background Printing

Include with Document
- ☐ Summary Info
- ☐ Field Codes
- ☐ Annotations
- ☐ Hidden Text
- ☒ Drawing Objects

Options for Current Document Only
- ☐ Print Data Only for Forms

Default Tray: From Control Panel ⬇

OK

Cancel

Help

Starting Word at turn-on

If you use Word just about every time you turn on your computer, you can set it up to start Word automatically. You do this in the Windows Program Manager

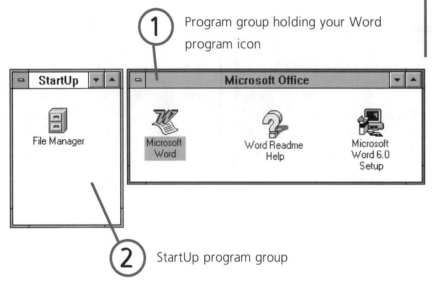

① Program group holding your Word program icon

② StartUp program group

③ Copy Program Item dialog box

④ From the drop-down list box, select StartUp

Basic steps:

1 In Program Manager open the group window which holds your Word icon (usually the Microsoft Office group window)

2 Open the StartUp group window

3 Click once on the Word program icon, then choose **File→Copy**, or type [Alt]+[F] then [C], or type [F8]. This calls up the Copy Program Item dialog box

4 Click on the To Group drop-down list box to display the groups available. Scroll through the list and select StartUp

Tip:

This action copies the Word program icon to the StartUp group window. Now, whenever you restart your computer Word will automatically startup. If you want this *not* to happen, simply delete the icon again

Shortcut keys

A great many things you do in Word, you do a great many times. Some of these things can be called upon with the click of a button on a toolbar, or a shortcut key command. Although buttons are a boon over choosing a command through the ordinary menu method, undoubtedly shortcut keys are the quickest.

At first sight, you might think not all commands are available as shortcuts. However, you can assign your own shortcut key commands to *any* command available in Word.

Basic steps:

1 Choose **Tools↪Customize**, or type ⌐Alt⌐+⌐T⌐ then ⌐C⌐, to call up the Customize dialog box

2 Click the Keyboard tab if it's not already frontmost

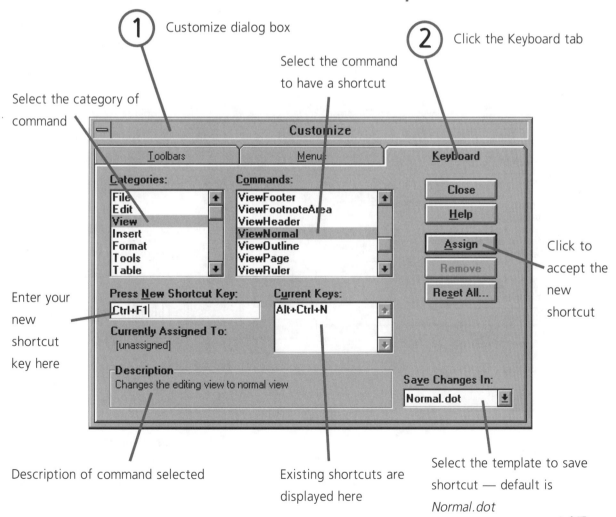

① Customize dialog box

Select the command to have a shortcut

② Click the Keyboard tab

Select the category of command

Click to accept the new shortcut

Enter your new shortcut key here

Description of command selected

Existing shortcuts are displayed here

Select the template to save shortcut — default is *Normal.dot*

147

Toolbars

While Word has a large number of toolbars, they may not always be to a user's liking. Either they might have the wrong buttons on for your particular tasks, or they might not have the buttons you want at all.

You can customize toolbars (by adding, deleting, changing and moving around buttons), and you can create your own toolbars (designing buttons from scratch if you want). You can also choose from a wide range of built-in buttons to assign to commands in Word.

ADAPTING A TOOLBAR

1 Choose
Tools↪Customize, or type ⎡Alt⎤+⎡T⎤ then ⎡C⎤, to call up the Customize dialog box

2 Click the Toolbars tab if it's not already frontmost

3 Drag a button onto the toolbar of your choice to add it (or drag a button *off* a toolbar to delete it)

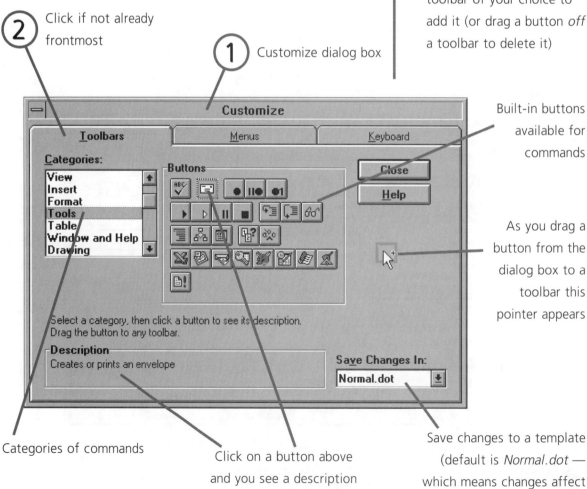

② Click if not already frontmost

① Customize dialog box

Built-in buttons available for commands

As you drag a button from the dialog box to a toolbar this pointer appears

Categories of commands

Click on a button above and you see a description of its command here

Save changes to a template (default is *Normal.dot* — which means changes affect all your Word documents)

148

CREATING A TOOLBAR

1 Choose
   View→Toolbars, or
   type **Alt**+**V** then then
   T, to call up the Toolbars
   dialog box

2 Click New, to call up the
   New Toolbar dialog box

3 Give the new toolbar a
   name

4 Click OK — the new
   toolbar is displayed as a
   floating toolbar on the
   screen and the Customize
   dialog box is called up
   with the Toolbars tab
   already frontmost (see
   below)

5 Drag buttons and adapt
   your new toolbar as before

Tip:

You can move (or delete) a toolbar button without the Customize dialog box. Just hold down **Alt** and drag the button to its new location (or drag it off the toolbar altogether to delete it). If you hold down **Alt** + **Ctrl** while you drag, the button is copied

Drag selected buttons to your toolbar

Drag your toolbar wherever you want it to be

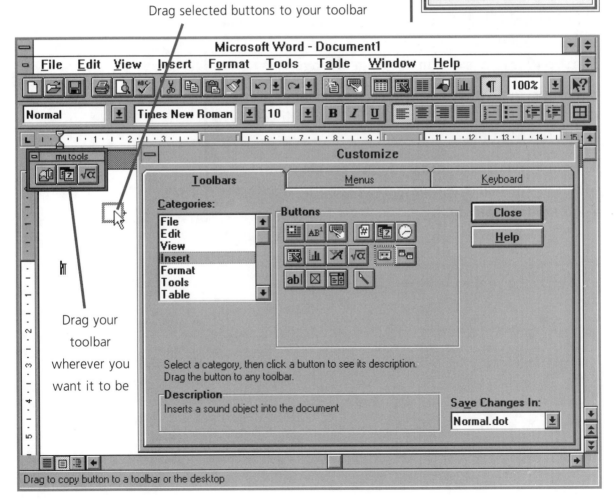

Summary for Section 7

● Before printing, preview your work in Print Preview. This way you save some paper finding out where your overall problems are.

● Use the Print dialog box to adjust controls regarding the pages you print, the number of copies you want, and so on.

● Use the Options dialog box with the Print tab frontmost to adjust finer details of printing.

● Use the Print button to print without any dialog boxes.

● Startup Word automatically each time you turn on your computer by copying Word's program icon to the StartUp program group in Program Manager.

● Assign your own shortcut keys to commands you use a lot through the Customize dialog box, with the Keyboard tab frontmost.

● Adapt existing toolbars, and create your own toolbars, through the Customize dialog box, with the Toolbars tab frontmost.

Index